CAE

WORKBOOK

ADVANTAGE

ROY KINGSBURY

FELICITY O'DELL • GUY WELLMAN

 LONGMAN

	STYLE AND REGISTER	READING	WRITING
1	Recognising styles in speech and in writing	Matching (part-)sentences with gaps in a text	Rewriting hotel notices/regulations in more informal English
2	Producing parallel formal and informal 'speech'	Matching linkers with gaps in a text / Deducing meaning from context	Expanding notes into complete lines from letters
3		Problem-solving and matching exercise	Rewriting a text using suggested changes
4	'Translating' journalese into a neutral style		Expanding (lecture) notes into complete sentences
5	'Translating' colloquial speech into standard written English	Modified cloze task / Locating information in paragraphs	Writing an opinion letter to a newspaper
	PROGRESS TEST 1 (Units 1–5)		
6		Matching statements with reasons / Matching words that rhyme	Writing an article about an oil tanker accident (from a variety of quotes)
7	'Translating' formal (written) to informal (spoken), and vice versa	Ordering a jumbled text	Writing a letter of advice in reply to the Reading text letter
8	'Translating' non-standard English into standard English	Matching sayings, proverbs and quotations with definitions	Rewriting a text using suggested changes
9		Matching halves of sentences	Writing about a child prodigy from notes
10		Re-ordering a jumbled text	Writing complete sentences from reference book notes
	PROGRESS TEST 2 (Units 6–10)		
11		Proofreading, suggesting simpler words / phrases, and True/False	Expanding notes into questions for a questionnaire
12	Euphemisms e.g. *less than fresh = stale*	Matching products (in a text) with advertising slogans	A letter of complaint to a company about its advertising
13	Choosing the correct formal phrases to replace informal ones	Completing a text with strongly collocating words (idioms)	Writing an account of a touring holiday (from visual prompts)
14		Matching (part-)sentences with gaps in an article	Writing an article from notes
15	Expressions in informal argument: *As I see it*, etc.	Deciding the order of race finishers from a sports article	Writing an entry for a competition to be a sports journalist
	PROGRESS TEST 3 (Units 11–15)		
16		Explaining headlines / Unscrambling a text	Writing a letter of advice about how to keep healthy abroad
17	Using phrasal verb nouns in place of phrasal verbs	Combined Reading and Writing task. Read an article, re-arrange discussion notes, and then write agreeing or disagreeing	
18	Completing a more formal version of an informal text		Writing a polite letter of complaint about damaged/unacceptable goods
19		Reading and re-ordering instructions / Deleting unnecessary words in a text	Writing precise instructions on how to do something
20	'Translating' informal thoughts into acceptable written forms and vice versa	Matching (part-) sentences with gaps in a text	Writing an article ('The Road to the Future') from notes
	PROGRESS TEST 4 (Units 16–20)		

Introduction

Aims of the Workbook

The Workbook is designed to revise and extend the language covered in *CAE Advantage* Coursebook. It offers further practice in grammar, vocabulary, reading, writing, and style and register, allowing you to reinforce and develop your skills in these key areas.

Structure of the Workbook

The Workbook contains twenty Units with a Progress Test after Units 5, 10, 15 and 20.

The Units and exercises

The Units offer a range of exercises and activities designed to give balanced and varied practice.

Each Workbook Unit consolidates by drawing together language and skills from different parts of the corresponding Coursebook Unit. You may, therefore, prefer to begin a Workbook Unit when you have covered most of the items in the relevant Coursebook Unit. Many grammar exercises will also encourage you to make further use of the Coursebook Grammar Commentary, and reading through the appropriate sections of this beforehand will help you.

With most exercises, space is provided for you to mark or write in your answers. Where this is not practical, the instructions will ask you to use a separate piece of paper which you may wish to keep on file for reference or revision.

Where appropriate, exercises begin with an example (labelled 0) in order to make it quite clear what you have to do.

Progress Tests

Each Progress Test is designed to allow you to check how well you have mastered the language practised in the preceding five Units. The Tests also reflect the kinds of tasks included in the Reading, Writing and English in Use Papers of the CAE Examination itself. Each Test should take approximately 100 minutes (1 hour 40 minutes) to complete and may be done over one or more lessons or 'sittings', if you are studying independently, according to your timetable. You can best measure your progress if you don't 'have a quick look' beforehand. Wait until you have completed the preceding five Units and then really 'test yourself'!

Using a dictionary

The Workbook generally encourages you to make use of a dictionary. Some exercises help you to develop your dictionary skills independently by introducing related vocabulary which you study in the context of a particular topic. However, try not to use a dictionary when doing a Progress Test.

1 It's a small world

Grammar

A In some of the sentences below there is an error in word order. Circle the word in the wrong place and draw an arrow to indicate where the word should be. Tick (✓) any sentences that are correct.

0 (Always) they spend their holidays in the same place.   . . . . .

1 I go often abroad on business.   . . . . .

2 Rarely did we meet anyone else on the beach.   . . . . .

3 Our car is breaking down always.   . . . . .

4 The weather is usually good there in July.   . . . . .

5 Generally, large hotels are the same throughout the world.   . . . . .

6 As a young girl I would read often travel books.   . . . . .

B Fill in the gap with the correct form of the verb in brackets at the end of the sentence.

0 It's hard to get used to . . . *driving* . . . . on the left in Britain. (drive)

1 He never used to . . . . so badly. (behave)

2 It was difficult at first but I am used to . . . . here now. (live)

3 I'm sure I'll never get used to . . . . here. (work)

4 What did you use to . . . . after school when you were a kid? (do)

5 She was used to . . . . several miles a day so she easily won the race. (run)

6 I used to . . . . sorry for him but I don't any more. (feel)

7 I can't get used to . . . . a big meal first thing in the morning. (have)

8 There didn't use to . . . . so many fast-food restaurants here. (be)

Vocabulary

C Write two more words or phrases which collocate with each of the words or phrases below.

0 a jar of olives, a jar of . . *jam* . . . ., a jar of . . *coffee* . . . . . .

1 a foreign accent, a/an . . . . accent, a/an . . . . accent

2 the human race, the . . . . race, the . . . . race

3 to save water resources, to . . . . water resources, to . . . . water resources

4 to gain weight, to . . . . weight, to . . . . weight

5 to put forward an idea, to put forward a/an . . . ., to put forward a/an . . . .

6 a highly trained employee, a/an . . . . trained employee, a/an . . . . trained employee

Reading

D Read the text below. There are gaps in it. Which of the options printed under the text fits into each gap? Three of the options do not fit.

It is hard to imagine that a hundred years ago a typical British summer holiday — (0) ..*C*... — would have been a day trip to the nearest beach. The rich and aristocratic perhaps did an occasional tour of the spas and ruins of Europe but only the most intrepid explorer (1)........

For many British people now the seaside day trip has been replaced by a fortnight on the Costa Brava or a Greek island. For many others (2)........ In the last year or so various acquaintances of mine — (3)...... — have been touring in Papua New Guinea, snorkelling in the Caribbean, admiring ancient sites in Peru, walking in the Canadian Rockies, enjoying the shops and night-life of Hong Kong, (4)......., looking at wild life in Siberia and even trekking in Bhutan.

It is probably truer than ever now to say to a young person that 'the world is your oyster'. A Londoner can (5)...... in the time it took him to reach the English Channel last century. In two days one can reach the other side of the world at a fare that is accessible (6)...... but to many people prepared to make a few sacrifices for the sake of travel.

However, no sooner does an adventurous traveller discover a new beauty spot or a picturesque town (7)........ Ostensibly their aim is to open up these new-found wonders to groups of holiday-makers in search of something different; in practice, they make what was once exotic into a tourist destination with the hotels, facilities and types of food (8)........ Perhaps it might be more accurate to say to the young traveller 'the world is your hamburger'.

a	than the package tour operators come along
b	fly to the Mediterranean
c ✓	for the majority of the population
d	particular to that area
e	living in Fiji
f	went further afield
g	found in all other tourist centres
h	exploring Burkina Faso
i	none of them rich or aristocratic
j	stayed at home
k	their destination is even more exotic
l	not just to the wealthy

Style and register

E Where might you expect to see or hear each of the following? Try and describe the language used. You may want to use some of these words.

> colloquial literary written neutral spoken informal formal contractions vocabulary grammar

0 **Beethoven, Ludwig van (1770–1827)** Great German composer. Wrote orchestral, choral and chamber music. Major works include nine symphonies, numerous piano concertos and sonatas and an opera, *Fidelio*.

Formal; encyclopedia (characteristic layout, basic facts stated in a neutral style)

1 Trespassers will be prosecuted.

. . . .

. . . .

2 I couldn't believe my eyes — I certainly hadn't expected to bump into anyone I knew in such a dreadful place on the other side of the world from my home.

. . . .

. . . .

3 Enjoy magnificent views from your balcony. Aquamarine sea abundant with spectacular tropical fish. Golden sands fringed by softly waving palm trees.

. . . .

. . . .

4 As an international consortium, we are in a perfect position to offer clients invaluable advice and assistance regarding profitable investments worldwide.

. . . .

. . . .

Writing

F Rewrite these hotel notices and regulations in more informal English so that guests find them friendlier. Write your friendlier notices on a separate piece of paper.

0 ■ On the day of departure guests are requested to vacate their rooms by noon.

Please leave your room before midday on your last day at the hotel.

1 ■ **Please refrain from smoking in bed.**

2 ■ Guests may dine in their rooms for a small surcharge.

3 ■ Morning calls must be requested before 10 p.m. on the preceding evening.

4 ■ Guests are strongly advised to deposit their valuables at reception.

2 *What's in a word?*

Grammar

A Circle the forms listed which can be used to complete each sentence. You may be able to circle more than one of the options.

0 You . . . . sleep in our spare room after the party next Saturday.

(a could) (b can) (c will be able to) (d would be able to) e were able to

1 I wish I . . . . speak Russian like you.

a can b could c had been able to d were able to e would be able to

2 In other circumstances, I . . . . you.

a would be able to help b had been able to help c could have helped d was able to help e would have been able to help

3 Although the cases were very heavy, I . . . . carry them there.

a could b was able to c have been able to d would be able to e couldn't

4 Since I came here, I . . . . relax.

a was able to b could c can d haven't been able to e couldn't

B On a separate piece of paper make four sentences with each list of prompts, using *should(n't) have (done)*, *could(n't) have (done)*, *might (not) have (done)* and *would(n't) have (done)*. You will have to re-order the prompts first.

0 climb better / not break leg / wear stronger shoes / not fall

You should have worn stronger shoes.
(Then) you could have climbed better.
You might not have fallen.
(And then) you wouldn't have broken your leg.

1 win the race / train harder / get the gold medal / run faster

2 able to borrow it from me / not get into trouble / not steal the money / borrow it

3 not buy a new car / be just as reliable / save a lot of money / buy a second-hand one

4 earn more than you do as a teacher / not give up the piano / be good enough to turn professional / become a really good player

C On a separate piece of paper, re-express this student's questions, using the word 'wish'.

0 Why aren't I better at English?

I wish I was (or were) better at English.

1 Why has English got so many different words for the same thing?

2 Why didn't I concentrate more in those early years of studying?

3 Why can't I imitate English intonation patterns better?

4 Why am I sitting here doing these exercises and not lazing on the beach?

5 Why won't somebody explain to me the difference between 'speak' and 'talk'?

6 Why aren't there clearer rules about preposition usage?

Vocabulary

D Find the correct form of the pairs of words in brackets to complete the sentence.

0 Apologies for any (offend / cause).   *offence caused*

1 Gaelic is still quite (wide / speak).   ....

2 They gained a (substance / percent) of the vote.   ....

3 Is there a (logic / connect) between spelling and pronunciation?   ....

4 Find three words that have the same (grammar / associate).   ....

5 We are hoping to promote (effect / learn).   ....

6 I think the whole thing is (absolute / ridicule)!   ....

Style and register

E Below are two very similar conversations; the main difference is that **1** is quite informal (two friends perhaps) and **2** is a lot more formal (maybe student and tutor). Complete them both (on a separate piece of paper) by expanding the prompts into complete sentences, as in the examples.

1

A: What / you / really / good?
What are you really good at?

B: not bad / history.

A: What / you / really / bad?

B: Well / a bit hopeless / maths.

A: What / particular problems with / maths?

B: I / never seem / enough time / so / not normally manage / finish / work.
I / just about cope / simple sums but / just / not get / point / algebra.

A: think / you / do with / more confident.

2

A: What / real strengths?
What are your real strengths?

B: think / certain aptitude / history.

A: What / weaknesses?

B: no real flair / mathematics.

A: What difficulties / experience / mathematics?

B: I / always find / insufficient time / this reason I rarely succeed / complete / assignments. I / normally able / handle basic arithmetic; however / fail / see / point / most algebraic equations.

A: feel / you suffer / lack / confidence.

Writing

F Using the prompts below, make complete sentences (on a separate piece of paper) for six different formal letters you've been asked to write. They are not connected.

0 you / so kind / complete / return / enclosed form / delay?

Would you be so kind as to complete and return the enclosed form without delay?

1 I / grateful / you / send / latest catalogue / price lists.

2 It / of great help / you / let us have / further details.

3 I / really / appreciate / you / let me know / end of this week.

4 we / ask / you / fax / information / as possible?

5 wonder / possible / you / inform / your decision / very near future.

6 Perhaps / you / kind enough / provide / us / exact numbers / Friday / latest.

Reading

G Read this text about Australian English and then do the two exercises below.

In Britain one can tell a great deal about a person from accent, (0)...*g*..., of course, the region or, even more specifically, the town of origin. In Australia, (1)......, amazing though it
5 may seem, there is very little regional variation in accent. For all the country's enormous area, there is little to distinguish the speech of citizens of Perth, Melbourne, or the far north. (2)...... odd words might be pronounced differently in
10 Canberra and Alice Springs and there are occasional items of vocabulary which are not used nationwide. (3)......, though, that Australian English can only really be divided into three broad categories. The first is called
15 Broad Australian, the second General

Australian and (4)...... there is Cultivated Australian, reserved for barely a tenth of the populace. (5)......, unlike the British, who have come to expect a certain accent from,
20 shall we say, Conservative Prime Ministers, London street sellers, Scottish footballers and Dorset farmers, Australians have some difficulty in pigeon-holing a fellow-countryperson in terms of class or
25 occupation, simply by the way they speak. And (6)...... English people commonly disguise their true accent or adopt a new one in order to conform to an image they want to cultivate, such a practice in Australia would
30 be unheard of. Top schools, boardrooms and government ministries have a full range of the three Australian 'languages' mentioned above. (7)......, next time you meet a perfect stranger from Australia, you'll have to ask a
35 lot if you want some background information; his or her voice will tell you very little.

1 The following words and phrases have been removed from the text. Where do they go? Match the letters with the numbers above.
a so **b** finally **c** however **d** whereas **e** the fact remains **f** furthermore **g** not least ✓ **h** of course

2 Which of the two 'translations' of these phrases from the text is more accurate in this context? Circle **a** or **b**.
for all (l.6) = **a** because of   **b** despite
odd (l.9) = **a** strange   **b** occasional
broad (l.14) = **a** approximate
             b geographically extensive
disguise (l.27) = **a** try to hide   **b** show pride in
cultivate (l.29) = **a** plant   **b** develop
practice (l.29) = **a** training   **b** habit
top schools (l.30) = **a** leading schools
             b high schools
perfect (l.33) = **a** ideal   **b** complete

3 It's a fact!

Grammar

A Which of these words or phrases fit in the gaps in these sentences? Circle those which do. You may find you circle all of them or just a few!

1 It was . . . . that he had stolen the money.

   a rumoured **b** thought **c** reported **d** hinted **e** suspected **f** known **g** believed **h** learned **i** suggested

2 He was . . . . to have stolen the money.

   a rumoured **b** thought **c** reported **d** hinted **e** suspected **f** known **g** believed **h** learned **i** suggested

3 . . . . he had finished one drink, he ordered another.

   a Once **b** Before **c** While **d** No sooner **e** As soon as **f** After **g** When **h** By the time **i** Until

4 In the end he was . . . . to sign the cheque.

   a convinced **b** persuaded **c** made **d** allowed **e** let **f** discovered **g** forbidden

5 I saw a man . . . . into the river.

   a had fallen **b** fall **c** to fall **d** fell **e** falling **f** having fallen **g** fallen **h** to have fallen

B Complete this passage with a suitable form of a verb of your choice. Write your answers on a separate piece of paper.

I (0) **had been acting** semi-professionally for ten years, but I (1). . . . . never . . . . Hamlet, or ever (2). . . . . of doing so. I (3). . . . . from nerves for days and while I (4). . . . . in the wings, I (5). . . . . my knees (6). . . . . 'Two minutes, everybody!' someone (7). . . . . I (8). . . . . down, (9). . . . . off my rather uncomfortable slippers and absent-mindedly (10). . . . . on my stage shoes. Just as I (11). . . . . up again, (12). . . . . deeply, the curtain (13). . . . . up. My big moment (14). . . . . ! I (15). . . . . (no sooner) . . . . one step forward than I (16). . . . . myself (17). . . . . on my back on the floor. In my panic I (18). . . . . my shoelaces together. I (19). . . . . quite still on the stage and (20). . . . . to 500 people (21). . . . . their heads off. I (22). . . . . (never) . . . . so embarrassed. And that, (23). . . . . it or not, (24). . . . . how my career as a comedian (25). . . . .

C Complete the following conversations using the prompts as in the example. Choose carefully between simple and continuous forms.

0   A: The boss was late this morning.

B: Yes, *he must have overslept.* . . . . (oversleep)

C: Not necessarily. . . . . *He might have been working*

at home. . . . . (work at home)

1   A: He was out of breath when he arrived.

B: Yes, ... (run)

C: Not necessarily. . . . .

. . . . (push his car)

2   A: He was in a foul temper.

B: Yes, ... (baby cry all night)

C: Not necessarily. . . . .

. . . . (have some bad news)

3   A: His eyes were all red.

B: Yes, ...

. . . . (drink last night)

C: Not necessarily. . . . .

. . . . (catch a cold)

4   A: He had blood on his chin.

B: Yes, ...

. . . . (cut himself shaving)

C: Not necessarily. . . . .

. . . . (fight with someone)

Writing

Use 'may' and 'must'

Get rid of 'that'; no 'which', either!

Use 'age of 25' / Use 'whose'

Use 'failed'

Use verbs not nouns; begin 'Not only'

Make this passive / Use 'was considered'

Use 'such'

Use 'enough' / Use 'according to'

Use 'later'

Again make passive

D A colleague has written a film review for the company newsletter. Your boss is not satisfied and wants you to rewrite it with her suggestions (left). Rewrite the piece on a separate piece of paper.

Perhaps you've seen and anyway no doubt you've heard of *Citizen Kane*, the classic film that was made by Orson Welles when he was 25. It was the story of a multi-millionaire who lived a life of extreme luxury but couldn't find happiness.

Welles was the director and writer as well as the star. When they first showed the film, in 1941, the critics all called it 'a truly remarkable achievement for one so young'.

Even today, amazing as it may seem, many experts think it is the best film ever made and, after 50 years, cinemas around the world are still regularly showing the film.

Vocabulary

Reading

A 'On the contrary!'

B 'I shall hear in heaven.'

C 'They couldn't hit an elephant at this dist—!'

D 'Does nobody understand?'

E 'More light!' ✓

F 'I've never felt better.'

G 'Die, my dear doctor, that's the last thing I shall do.'

H 'Either that wallpaper goes, or I do.'

I 'All my possessions for one moment of time.'

J 'Mozart!'

K 'I am just going outside, and I may be some time.'

THIS IS MY LAST W__!

E Sort these words into five groups of five, according to theme. Write them on a separate piece of paper and choose a heading for each group.

0 *Dishonest behaviour: con, gullible, swindle, victim, suspicious*

reward	swindle ✓	receipt	caterpillar	clerk
goat	lease	victim ✓	suspicious ✓	butterfly
con ✓	beetle	contractor	widow	groom
warden	bride	witness	deposit	porter
gullible ✓	cattle	psychiatrist	registrar	debt

F Read this passage and decide where each of the quotations on the left belongs. Match the letters with the numbers.

A selection of famous people's dying words can make interesting reading. All human life is there, the heroic, the witty, the banal: the German poet Goethe's two urgent monosyllables (0) . . .*E*. . . , the deaf composer Beethoven's touching confidence in regaining his aural faculties in the next world (1) . . . . . . , the Irish writer James Joyce's final frustration and despair (2) . . . .

What state of mind shall we be in when we depart this life? Will we be brief like Mahler, calling out to his fellow composer (3) . . . . . . ? Will we go with a joke and a pun (presumably intentional) like the statesman Lord Palmerston (4) . . . . . . ? Or will we say farewell bravely like Captain Lawrence Oates (5) . . . . . . , as he sacrificed his own life in the freezing wasteland to offer his fellow Antarctic explorers a chance of survival? No. More likely we shall pass some mundane, domestic comment about the bedroom décor like the witty writer Oscar Wilde (6) . . . . . . — but unfortunately without his wit!

I like the plea of Queen Elizabeth I, willing to sacrifice everything for a little longer on this earth (7) . . . . But my personal favourites are the last words of the Norwegian playwright Henrik Ibsen contradicting a friend's assurance that he was getting better (8) . . . . . . and those of poor John Sedgewick, the American Civil War general, who fatally disregarded advice not to look over the parapet at the enemy, saying (9) . . . . And best of all perhaps: the actor Douglas Fairbanks' ironic claim to be feeling just great (10) . . . . What a way to go!

4 News of the world

Vocabulary

A In the text below, choose the correct word to fill each of the gaps from the words listed beneath the text.

> The newspaper with the largest (0) ..*a*... in the United Kingdom is *The Sun,* bought by over four million people every day. *The Sun* is a (1)....... newspaper and it is more interested in (2)....... about the royal family and film stars than in real news about, (3)......., government policies or foreign (4)....... There are more (5)....... national newspapers than quality papers in the UK. One of the most (6)....... read of the quality papers is *The Daily Telegraph* which is generally (7)....... in its political (8).......

0	(a) circulation	b issue	c edition	d number
1	a tabular	b table	c tabloid	d tablet
2	a sayings	b stories	c gossips	d myths
3	a tell	b say	c imagine	d suppose
4	a subjects	b points	c affairs	d topics
5	a popular	b quantity	c rubbish	d mass
6	a strongly	b broadly	c widely	d heavily
7	a right-hand	b right-angled	c right-minded	d right-wing
8	a propaganda	b opinions	c meanings	d critics

B These words are all verbs. First write down any preposition which usually follows the verb. Then write (a) one noun and (b) one adjective based on the same root — and underline the syllable with the main stress. Use a dictionary if necessary.

0 retain *No prep. (a) retention, (b) retentive* ....

1 suspect ....

2 compliment ....

3 insist ....

4 argue ....

5 stress ....

6 regret ....

7 establish ....

8 allege ....

9 agree ....

10 believe ....

Grammar

C Look at these quotations about the news. Put each quotation into reported speech beginning with the words provided below. Write your answers on a separate piece of paper.

We welcome almost any break in the monotony of things, and a man has only to murder a series of wives in a new way to become known to millions of people who have never heard of Homer.
(Robert Lynd, Anglo-Irish journalist)

Newspapers are so filthy and bestial that no honest man would admit one into his house for a water closet doormat.
(Charles Dickens, 19th-century English novelist)

Never believe in mirrors or newspapers.
(John Osborne, English playwright)

When a dog bites a man, that is not news but when a man bites a dog, that is news.
(John Bogart, American journalist)

The American reading his Sunday paper in a state of lazy collapse is perhaps the most perfect symbol of the triumph of quantity over quality… Whole forests are being ground into pulp to minister to our triviality.
(Irving Rabbit)

In those days we had a real political democracy led by a hierarchy of statesmen and not a fluid mass distracted by newspapers.
(Winston Churchill, British statesman)

It is part of the social mission of every great newspaper to provide a refuge and a home for the largest possible number of salaried eccentrics.
(Lord Thomson, Canadian newspaper publisher)

Journalism consists largely of saying 'Lord Jones dead' to people who never knew that Lord Jones was alive.
(G. K. Chesterton, English writer)

0 Winston Churchill maintained *that in those days people had had a real political democracy led by statesmen and not a fluid mass distracted by newspapers.*

1 Robert Lynd felt …

2 John Bogart admitted …

3 Charles Dickens insisted …

4 John Osborne warned …

5 Lord Thomson declared …

6 G. K. Chesterton pointed out …

7 Irving Rabbit wrote …

D Finish each of these sentences in such a way that it means the same as the sentence printed before it.

0 'You students started the fight,' said the president.

The president accused *the students of starting the fight.*

1 It's common knowledge that he has been in prison several times.

He is known . . . .

. . . .

2 'Let's write to the editor,' my sister said.

My sister suggested . . . .

. . . .

3 'Please reconsider your decision,' said the workers.

The workers begged the boss . . . .

. . . .

4 According to today's paper, he is planning a new film version of Robin Hood.

He is rumoured . . . .

. . . .

5 'I hate to be criticised by non-professionals,' the film star said.

The film star objected . . . .

. . . .

6 'You conducted a marvellous interview,' they said to the reporter.

The reporter was congratulated . . . .

. . . .

7 People say that he is a millionaire.

He is reputed . . . .

. . . .

8 There are reports that she killed her husband.

She is alleged . . . .

. . . .

Style and register

E The items below are in the style of popular journalism — headlines and sentences. On a separate piece of paper rewrite them in a more straightforward or neutral style.

0 MP quits over cash blunder

A Member of Parliament has resigned because of an error concerning money.

1 Key information on a possible boardroom shake-up came to light yesterday.

2 Twenty Britons have been booted out of Uclesia as a result of a diplomatic feud.

3 The President vowed to curb government spending yesterday.

4 Local football team trounced in last night's match

5 Government slammed as number of jobless hits all-time high

6 Share prices plummeted yesterday in response to Finance Ministry leaks.

Writing

F Below are some notes taken at a lecture. Rewrite them as complete sentences on a separate piece of paper.

0 John Tusa — head — BBC World Service — number — years.

John Tusa was head of the BBC World Service for a number of years.

1 British government — set up — World Service — international voice — Britain overseas — aim — bind Empire together.

2 Aims change every decade — 30s desire: bind Empire — 40s anti-fascist propaganda — 50s Cold War — 60s de-colonisation.

3 World Service today — broadcast — 36 languages — almost every part — world.

4 Variety — programmes — news — sport — art — religion — science.

5 Receive frequent requests — start — broadcast more languages e.g. Sinhala.

Out of this world

Grammar

A Expand these notes into sentences. Use the verbs *look, sound, smell, taste* or *feel* as given, with an adjective, with *like* or with *as if/as though*.

0   That hat / terrible on you! You / idiot! (look)
That hat looks terrible on you! You look like an idiot!

1   He / very apologetic yesterday. He / just / his father. (sound)

. . . .

2   She / so pale when she arrived. She / see a ghost. (look)

. . . .

3   This new perfume / dreadful. It / old socks! (smell)

. . . .

4   You / worried. You / have bad news. (sound)

. . . .

5   After the operation, I / quite ill. I / hit by a lorry! (feel)

. . . .

6   The soup / awful! It / soap, not soup! (taste)

. . . .

7   The coffee they gave us / fine, but it / made last week! (smell, taste)

. . . .

B Choose an appropriate verb from those in the box and supply the correct infinitive form in the blanks — *to do, to be doing, to have done* or *to have been doing*.

There was an eerie atmosphere in the house. The ancient walls themselves appeared (0) **to breathe** evil, and the breath from the walls was rotten. I seemed (1) . . . . along endless corridors for hours when the candle in my hand went out. I shuddered. Although I felt nothing, it seemed (2) . . . . by a sharp blast of wind — and I was left in darkness. 'It seems (3) . . . . colder,' I thought to myself, and shuddered again. Suddenly there was a voice that appeared (4) . . . . from above. It was a man's voice, deep and threatening. 'You seem (5) . . . . your way,' the voice said.

| get | lose | breathe | be blown out | wander | come |

Vocabulary

C Choose any appropriate words from this box, and form plurals to complete the blanks. Not all the words will be needed.

spacecraft	mouse	tooth	child	sheep	trout	louse
deer	goldfish	criterion	goose	phenomenon	aircraft	
analysis	cactus	basis				

0 That man grows . . . *cacti* . . . . . and breeds . *goldfish* . . . . . as a hobby.

1 . . . . have grey fur, very sharp . . . . and long tails.

2 Numerous . . . . of computer data have proved that many operators do not consider the . . . . by which they file information.

3 . . . . seem to breed easily in the hair of young . . . .

4 Pilots of jet . . . . have reported some very unusual . . . . over the North Pole recently.

5 The Americans sent up two . . . . last year.

D Combine words on the left with the suffixes on the right to make adjectives to fill the blanks.

air	water	idiot	car	-tight	-sick	-proof
shock	travel	home	child			
sound	sea					

0 Whenever I travel in an aeroplane, I get . *airsick* . . . .

1 You needn't worry if you drop that watch. It's . . . .

2 By the way, you can wear it swimming, too. It's . . . .

3 She's so . . . . that she rings her mother every day.

4 I think these . . . . caps they put on medicine bottles are great.

5 We put the cake in an . . . . container to keep it fresh.

Style and register

E This is part of what a teenager told a classmate of hers. It is in a very colloquial style. Read it and then, on a separate piece of paper, write the more acceptable or standard version that she wrote to an advice column in a magazine. Make sure that you replace all the words and phrases underlined, and make any other changes that seem appropriate. You may need to use a dictionary.

You might begin like this: *I get very annoyed with my parents …*

'I get really <u>fed up</u> with my parents always <u>picking holes in</u> everything I do. Yesterday my dad threatened to <u>chuck out</u> all my cassettes if I didn't tidy up my room. Then he just stood there <u>gawping</u> while I <u>slaved away</u> for ages <u>stuffing</u> things into drawers and onto shelves. It really <u>got on my nerves,</u> especially as instead of <u>pitching in to help</u>, he <u>kept going on about</u> my friends <u>dropping in</u> at all hours and me <u>chatting away</u> on the phone to them for ages.'

Reading

F Read this article and choose nine appropriate words from those below to fill in the blanks. Write the number of the blanks against the words you choose.

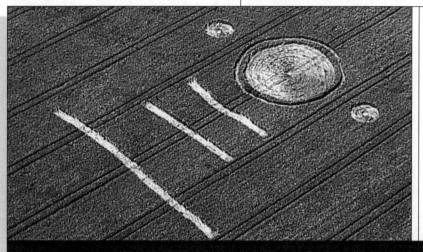

Crop circles: What on earth *are* they?

a You must have heard of them. They've been seen and recorded all over Europe — from England to Hungary, from Sweden to Bulgaria. Amateur and professional scientists alike have shown (0). . . . . interest in them, but they seem to have (1). . . . . everyone.

b Crop circles are large circles and other shapes that have appeared in fields of corn, wheat and other crops in different parts of Europe. They have aroused so much interest that in Sweden, for instance, a group of eminent scientists in 1991 launched a nationwide (2). . . . . into crop circles.

c People disagree about them, as they do about other strange (3). . . . . such as ghosts and UFOs. Unlike UFOs, however, they are certainly not the (4). . . . . of people's imagination: they are there for all to see.

d According to some, the formations or patterns on each (5). . . . . are the marks left by (6). . . . . piloted by (7). . . . . intelligences — so are we on the (8). . . . . of meeting other inhabitants of the Universe? For others, they are the result of unusual weather conditions; and for yet others, they are not only man-made, but made by hoaxers.

e Whatever they are, they have certainly provided many journalists with a good story!

phenomena ☐ site ☐ considerable **0** analysis ☐
threshold ☐ spacecraft ☐ mystified ☐ edge ☐
product ☐ extra-terrestrial ☐ investigation ☐

G Read the article again. Which paragraph

1 explains what crop circles are? ☐
2 suggests the circles could be made by aliens? ☐
3 tells us how widespread the phenomenon is? ☐
4 suggests they might be made by practical jokers? ☐
5 reports scientific research into the circles? ☐

Writing

H On a separate piece of paper write a short letter (say, 70 – 80 words) to the newspaper saying what *you* think the crop circles might possibly be. Make at least two suggestions. Begin your letter: 'Sir, I refer to the article on "Crop circles" that appeared in yesterday's edition of your newspaper.'

Progress Test 1 (Units 1-5)

SECTION A: WRITING

Time: 45 minutes

The last time you stayed with three friends, you all agreed it would be nice to spend a holiday together next spring, possibly in North Wales. This advertisement attracted you last weekend and you rang to make enquiries. While, and after, talking to UK Country Homes, you made some notes (below). Using the ad and your notes, write a letter telling your friends about the holiday and asking if you should book it. You should write about 200 words.
Write your answer on a separate piece of paper.

A
Great Way
to
Discover
The English Countryside!

— and the Scottish, Welsh and Northern Ireland countryside as well.

What better way to discover the countryside than to spend a fortnight in an old cottage or the wing of a country house or mansion? You can rent any of our properties from £100 per person✣ including all linen, gas and electricity. Write or phone for our free 90-page colour brochure featuring all our properties.

UK Country Homes

✣ Price based on group of four sharing a property

Call to UK Country Homes

— *All properties — minimum two-week let: 3rd week cheaper.*

— *Number of lovely old cottages in North Wales (near Snowdonia National Park) — very reasonable (£125 p.p. for 2 weeks, incl. hire car): only £10 p.p. deposit to secure.*

— *Sounds good — must decide when to go — need to book as early as poss! (I suggest 1st 2 weeks May.)*

— *North Wales cottages — great!*

Let's do it! — will get further details from brochure (in post). I'll pay any deposit for the moment.

SECTION B: READING

Suggested time: 15 minutes

Read this article and then, from the list **A-G** below, choose the most appropriate heading to summarise each of the five paragraphs. Two of the suggested paragraph headings will not apply.

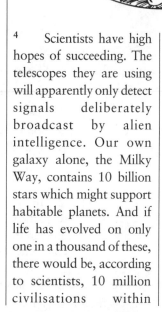

Earth Calling Space: 'Is There Anyone Out There?'

1   October 12, 1992 might turn out to be one of the great days in the history of mankind. If the search begun on that day is successful, it could herald a new era — or it could be the beginning of the end for the earth and its inhabitants.

2   That was the day on which the US space agency NASA launched a major new search for alien civilisations in space by aiming two powerful radio telescopes towards a small star in the constellation of Ophiuchus. It is a search which is planned to last ten years at a total cost of $100 million.

3   This is not the first time astronomers have searched the skies for signs of intelligent life, but it is certainly the most ambitious. Using two telescopes, NASA scientists are planning to scan the skies for any signs of life 'out there'. While one enormous telescope at the Arecibo Observatory in Puerto Rico will be trained on 1,000 nearby stars, another will search the rest of the sky. Data gathered from both sources will then be collected and analysed, and scientists will monitor the whole experiment as it progresses.

4   Scientists have high hopes of succeeding. The telescopes they are using will apparently only detect signals deliberately broadcast by alien intelligence. Our own galaxy alone, the Milky Way, contains 10 billion stars which might support habitable planets. And if life has evolved on only one in a thousand of these, there would be, according to scientists, 10 million civilisations within 130,000 light years.

5   That seems an enormous number, so if that is the case, why is it that we haven't picked up any 'Is there anyone out there?' messages ourselves from one of those 10 million civilisations? Science-fiction writers through the ages have nearly always assumed that extra-terrestrial civilisations would be more intelligent than our own. But if they're out there, *are* they? ∎

Possible paragraph headings

A Success guaranteed?

B Positive signals already

C Are We more intelligent than Them?

D Constellation Orion most likely

E A $100 million gamble?

F Data constantly to be analysed

G A historic day

Paragraph 1: ....

Paragraph 2: ....

Paragraph 3: ....

Paragraph 4: ....

Paragraph 5: ....

SECTION C: ENGLISH IN USE

Time: 40 minutes

1 Rewrite each of the following sentences beginning with the word or words given on the next line. Your rewritten version should mean exactly the same as the original.

1 People here rarely go shopping on Sundays.

Here it's rare . . . .

2 My father always used to take me fishing with him.

My father would . . . .

3 She can't get into the habit of studying every evening.

She can't get used . . . .

4 I regret not paying much attention to the lecture.

I wish . . . .

5 When she heard the news, she broke down.

On . . . .

6 Perhaps I didn't get a better job because I didn't study hard enough.

I might . . . .

7 It may seem strange, but I've never wanted to go to America.

Strange . . . .

8 She looks as if she's having a good time.

She seems . . . .

9 I can only assume you were holding the thing upside down.

You must . . . .

10 People know that she's living in France.

She's known . . . .

2 In most lines of this text there is one mistake with a verb tense. Read the text, underline each incorrect tense and write the correct tense in the space provided at the end of the line. Where a line is completely correct, put a tick (✓) against the line number.

When Rudolf Nureyev, the famous ballet dancer, had died on	1 . . . .
6th January, 1993, his friends said that he was ill for some	2 . . . .
time and that he suffered from AIDS for some months.	3 . . . .
Nureyev defected from the Leningrad Kirov Ballet in Paris in	4 . . . .
1961, and since that time has danced in almost every country	5 . . . .
in the world until he was retiring in 1992. In the months	6 . . . .
before his death, although he must go into hospital on	7 . . . .
repeated occasions, he still travelled widely between his	8 . . . .
homes in Italy, Paris, America and the Caribbean. He has been	9 . . . .
a great ambassador and will be sorely missed by ballet lovers	10 . . . .
everywhere.	

3   Report these short dialogues in one sentence each. Use the verbs given and complete the reports as begun, in the past.

1   HE: I've been listening to you on the phone.
         I heard everything!   (admit)

    SHE: Well, you're a hypocrite! (*pause*)
          But I'm sorry for what I did earlier.   (accuse / apologise)

    When he . . . .

    . . . .

    . . . .

2   SHE: *Please* think it over again. *I* will.   (implore / promise)

    THEY: All right, so will we. But don't
           expect too much.   (agree / warn)

    After she . . . .

    . . . .

    . . . .

3   HE: Remember, we've got to leave by six.
         Of course, we could try to leave earlier.   (remind / suggest)

    SHE: I'd forgotten the concert was tonight.
          Anyway, how can I possibly be ready
          that early?!   (confess / demand to know)

    When he . . . .

    . . . .

    . . . .

    . . . .

    . . . .

4   This is part of what a woman told a friend. Read it carefully. Then fill in the blanks in the (more formal) version that she wrote in a letter to a theatrical acquaintance of hers.
Do not write more than one word in any one space.

'I've always been very interested in acting, you know. So I've decided. And I'm going to let you in on my decision. I'm going to appear on TV! I don't want to offend anybody, of course, but I know I can act. People with a lot less ability than me have managed to get onto TV.'

I have always ⁽¹⁾. . . . . a great interest in acting. I have
⁽²⁾. . . . . a decision, and I wish to ⁽³⁾. . . . . it on
record. I am going to ⁽⁴⁾. . . . . an appearance on television!
Naturally I have no ⁽⁵⁾. . . . . to ⁽⁶⁾. . . . . offence to
anyone, but I am ⁽⁷⁾. . . . . that I have a ⁽⁸⁾. . . . . for
acting. People with ⁽⁹⁾. . . . . less ability have ⁽¹⁰⁾. . . . .
in getting onto television.

We're all in the same boat

Grammar

A Complete **b** and **c** each time so that they mean the same as sentence **a**.

0 a Do nothing, and the problem will get worse.

  b If we don't *do anything / something, the problem will get worse.*

  c Unless we *do something, the problem will get worse.*

1 a For this project we need global support.

  b The thing we . . . .

  c What is . . . .

2 a The situation has deteriorated because nothing was done earlier.

  b If something . . . .

  c Had . . . .

3 a Most people would approve of a ban on hunting.

  b If we were . . . .

  c Were there . . . .

4 a Why wasn't this taken into consideration 20 years ago?

  b This should . . . .

  c Someone ought . . . .

5 a Why can't we show these animals a little more respect?

  b It's about time we . . . .

  c It's high time these . . . .

6 a Perhaps it would have been possible to solve the problem before it became so serious.

  b The problem could probably . . . .

  c We might . . . .

7 a Millions of birds are dying unnecessarily, and that's tragic.

  b What . . . .

  c The fact . . . .

8 a We might be faced with famine on a massive scale.

  b What . . . .

  c Famine on a massive scale . . . .

Vocabulary

B Which of these words goes in which gap in the text below? Put each letter next to the appropriate number.

A number	D increase	G fallen	J reduce ✓
B to	E by	H doubled	K declining
C drop	F growing	I risen	L of

For years now conservationists and animal protection societies have been trying to (0) ...*J*.... the frequency of the killings but (1) .... numbers of poachers coupled with a substantial (2) .... in the value of ivory has led to the elephants' population (3) .... even further. Cases of the beasts simply disappearing from the reservation have almost (4) .... in (5) .... in just a couple of years. Their total population has now fallen (6) .... just over 200, which represents a (7) .... (8) .... over 60% in four years. In the past two years alone their numbers have declined (9) .... 70%.

The only encouraging sign is that the number of poaching prosecutions has (10) .... dramatically over the past twelve months and the number of seriously wounded and/or dying elephants found has recently (11) .... considerably.

Reading

C Sentences 0–9 were followed by sentences A–J in the original information leaflet about what YOU can do to help the environment. But which came after which? Match the letters with the numbers.

0 Nine-tenths of all rubbish can be recycled. ..*F*.

1 Make a point of driving less. ....

2 Keep CFCs right out of your home. ....

3 Try to cut your gas and electricity bills by half. ....

4 Water is precious. ....

5 Conserve heat. ....

6 Plant trees. ....

7 Don't use toxic chemical pesticides in the garden. ....

8 Take your own bags shopping with you. ....

9 Check what sort of plates you're being served on. ....

A This will help to absorb the carbon dioxide in the atmosphere.

B Make sure your house is properly insulated with windows double-glazed.

C Use public transport, share lifts, try two wheels or even two feet!

D Insist on proper ones rather than paper or plastic.

E Say no to unwanted packaging and packing.

F So don't just throw away paper, glass, aluminium and plastic indiscriminately. ✓

G Use pump products, not aerosols.

H Don't overheat water, use energy-efficient light bulbs and always turn off lights in rooms that aren't being used.

I Don't leave taps on unnecessarily — when rinsing dishes or cleaning your teeth, for example.

J Much less harmful ones can be just as effective.

D These are the missing words at the end of each line of the poem below. Which goes where? Match the numbers with the letters.

A brain	F blind	K began	P dwell
B bell	G rain	L mind	Q race ✓
C ill	H disease	M will	R CFCs
D speak	I face ✓	N wild	S tide
E suicide	J week	O Man	T smiled

ROGER WODDIS

Keep It Green

The trouble with the human (0)..*Q*..,
Which wears a smirk upon its (0)..*I*..
To indicate its massive (1).......,
Is being dumb and deaf and (2).......

It does not hear the warning (3).......
To all that on this planet (4).......,
It cannot see beyond this (5).......,
It has a tongue, but does not (6).......

The forest dies deprived of (7)....... ,
Lead damages the childish (8)....... ,
Pollution poisons turf and (9).......
And makes for global (10).......

We court disasters and (11)....... ,
And if, brought on by (12)....... ,
The Big Heat doesn't make us (13).......,
Be sure untreated water (14).......

The smallest creature in the (15).......,
The dinosaur that rarely (16).......
And roamed the earth when life (17).......
Is nowhere near as dumb as (18)....... .

* See note on inside front cover.

E What is the message of the poem? See if you can summarise it in two sentences.

Writing

F As a newspaper journalist, you made notes from interviews with people after an oil-tanker accident off a Canadian island. Use the notes you made below to write your article, reporting the gist of what the people said and adding any information you think useful or important. (Try not to use any one reporting verb like *say* or *deny* more than once.)

'You read about this sort of thing, but you never think it could happen to you. It really shouldn't happen in this day and age, should it? The air now is horrible, full of … I don't know … pollution, I suppose. It's horrific.' (*Resident of 25 years on the island*)

'The chemicals they're using will do as much damage as the oil itself. The winds they get up here would break it up naturally and any that escaped could be dispersed mechanically. Why only chemically? It's crazy.' (*Member of an environmental group*)

'We shall be holding a full enquiry, of course. No stone will be left unturned; you have my word on that.' (*A government spokesperson*)

'I shall be seeking compensation of course, and not just for what you can see has happened to my animals but also for what may have happened and nobody will see that for two, three, four years.' (*An island farmer*)

'The loss of wildlife is incalculable — not just the birds but the fish, otters, mice, millions of them. It's a tragedy.' (*A Canadian ornithologist*)

'No comment!' (*The oil-tanker captain*)

7 Just a phase they're going through

Reading

A This is a letter to 'Halina Swift's Problem Page' in a magazine, but the sentences are in the wrong order. Put them into the correct order. Number them 0–8 in the spaces.

Dear Halina,

a ... I shall probably be able to find something fairly easily in one of our local hotels and that will allow us to save up more quickly for a flat together. As soon as we can afford something we shall get married.

b ... I'd be very happy if my parents would only understand and approve of my decision. How can I persuade them that they are wrong? Please give me some advice.

c ... Let me put you in the picture by telling you that I am now in my last year at school and preparing hard for my final exams. I'm reasonably successful at school and my parents have always assumed that I'd go on to university.

d ... They also say that, in a few years' time, I shall wish I hadn't given up my studies.

e **0**. I have this tricky problem which I hope you'll help me solve.

f ... They argue that we have not known each other for long enough to know our own true feelings.

g ... To me this is a perfect plan and I have no regrets about not going to university. My parents, unfortunately, don't agree.

h ... Until recently so did I. However, a few weeks ago, I met someone I've fallen deeply in love with.

i ... We both agree that we were made for each other and that there is no point in our living apart. We have, therefore, decided that I should start work immediately after leaving school.

Yours,

Writing

B On a separate piece of paper, write a reply from Halina, referring to the points in the letter and giving the advice that you feel is most appropriate. Write about 150 words.

Vocabulary

C Divide these words into groups of (a) nouns, (b) verbs and (c) adjectives. Some words may fit into more than one group. Use a dictionary if you want to.

rebellious	rash	mumps	bully	tease
heartbroken	mock	unsightly	mop	blush
self-conscious	day-dreamer	poster	cheat	confiscate
common	glance	squint	sigh	clumsy
tingle	kid	teenager	nurse	cautious

D Which of the words from **C** fit best into the gaps in these sentences? If necessary, change the form of the words.

0 Although he is now a pillar of society, he was once expelled from school for ... *cheating* .... in his exams.

1 Don't just stand there looking at the spilt milk. Go and fetch a .... at once.

2 When the teacher saw me reading a comic in class, he .... it immediately.

3 Chickenpox is a childhood illness which brings the patient out in a ....

4 There is one boy in the class who is such a terrible .... that the other kids are afraid to go out in the playground when he's there.

5 When I .... out of the window, I was amazed to see how dark it was.

6 She has a large .... of Tom Cruise on her wall and she is always looking at it and .... deeply.

7 He could probably be prescribed some glasses to get rid of that ....

8 That's the third time you've knocked over that vase! Why are you so ....?

E Now write sentences using five more words from **C** that you especially want to learn.

Grammar

F Write sentences which have the same meaning as the sentence provided but use the word in brackets at the end of that sentence.

0 I don't approve of my brother smoking. (wish)
   I wish my brother didn't smoke. ....

1 I now regret turning down the job. (wish)

   ....

2 I am not sorry that I told him he was a bully. (regret)

   ....

3 I'll never forget meeting him for the first time. (remember)

. . . .

4 I wish I hadn't been so rebellious as a teenager. (regret)

. . . .

5 I'm sorry my father never told me more about his childhood. (wish)

. . . .

G In the paragraph below there are **ten** grammatical errors (including the example), all connected with verb forms. Underline the mistakes and write corrections for the remaining nine in the spaces.

. . . . ***do***	When I was a teenager I used to hate having to do homework. Our maths teacher seemed particularly to enjoy making us <u>to do</u> work over the weekend. I remember once not to do my preparation for a big Monday morning maths test because I had been too busy having a good time with my friends. So I played truant and went to the park with a friend instead of go to school. Unfortunately, the biology teacher decided that day to take a class to the park for collecting some plant samples. He saw me sitting in the park listen to my Walkman and, of course, he reported me to the school principal. You can't imagine the trouble I had been in! I had confiscated my Walkman. I was used to be in trouble with my teachers but this was, for some reason, considered worse than my previous misdemeanours. I was also made correct all my classmates' maths tests and I was told I was lucky not being expelled.

Style and register

H The language which a teacher might use when speaking to another teacher about a 10-year-old pupil is less formal and diplomatic than that which the same teacher might write to the pupil's parents in a school report. Complete the table below with expressions meaning approximately the same but in an appropriate style.

'John's a lazy little devil.'

0 ***John needs to apply himself more.***

1 . . . .

John's handwriting could be improved.

2 . . . .

John would benefit from paying more attention in class.

'John's usually at the centre of any trouble.'

3 . . . .

'John's pretty thick at times.'

4 . . . .

5 . . . .

Mathematics is not John's best subject.

'That John's really rude at times.'

6 . . . .

Rich man, poor man

Grammar

A Rewrite these sentences in two different ways, using the words or phrases given. Make any changes necessary. Write your answers on a separate piece of paper.

0 Financial problems often lead to the break-up of a family.
  a (stem from) *The break-up of a family often stems from financial problems.*
  b (a direct consequence) *The break-up of a family is often a direct consequence of financial problems.*

1 Bad management was the major cause of the collapse of the company.
  a (trace back to) **b** (the reason why)

2 Social injustices can be caused by government policies.
  a (have roots in) **b** (lead to)

3 The reasons why some people turn to crime are fairly easy to understand.
  a (the reasons for) **b** (it's)

4 Unemployment is often responsible for social problems.
  a (result from) **b** (lead to)

Vocabulary

B The answer to this puzzle is something that those with wealthy parents would like to avoid paying — but the word is spelt backwards. What is it? (Answers 1–14 read from top to bottom.)

1 Cost. Noun from which we get 'expensive'. (7)

2 Money and possessions. Anagram THE LAW. (6)

3 Take illegally. Anagram SLATE. (5)

4 One who invests money to make more money. (8)

5 Of a value too great to be described. Sounds as if it means 'without price'. (9)

6 Verb from 'economy'. (9)

7 Too valuable for worth to be measured. Re-order IN ABLE VALU(E). (10)

8 Calculate, guess. Anagram MEAT SITE. (8)

9 Amount of money you are charged for something. (5)

10 State of being poor. Anagram VERY TOP. (7)

11 When you write a cheque, you M___ it O__. (4, 3)

12 Plural noun from 'rich' = wealth. (6)

13 Give out money in payment. Re-order EDSNP. (5)

14 Money gained by a business. Anagram FOR TIP. (6)

Reading

A Money can't buy friends, but you can get a better class of enemy. (*Spike Milligan, English comedian and writer*)

C There are lots of sayings and quotations in English about money. What do the ones below mean? Match the sayings and quotations with the explanations. (Two of the sayings or quotations are not explained.)

B Money should circulate like rainwater. (*Thornton Wilder, 1897–1975, American playwright and novelist*)

C It has been said that the love of money is the root of all evil. The want of money is so quite as truly. (*Samuel Butler, 1835–1902, English satirist and novelist*)

D All money nowadays seems to be produced with a natural homing instinct for the Treasury.* (*His Royal Highness the Duke of Edinburgh, quoted in* The Observer, *1963*)

E And no one shall work for money, and no one shall work for fame, But each for the joy of the working. (*Rudyard Kipling, 1865–1936, English author*)

F Take care of the pence and the pounds will take care of themselves.

G The middle-class woman of England, as of America … think of her in bulk … is potentially the greatest money-spending machine in the world. (*H. Granville Barker, 1877–1946, English actor, playwright and producer*)

H You pays your money and you takes your choice. (*Punch magazine, 1846*)

I Money talks.

J A fool and his money are soon parted.

K Time is money.

0 In the future people will work because they love working rather than to earn money or to win glory. . .*E*. . . .

1 Money should be distributed equally among everyone. . . . .

2 One section of society spends money like no other. . . . .

3 There is a clear connection between money and crime. . . . .

4 If you've got money, you can always get something done, even if it seemed impossible at first. . . . .

5 Money is made by the government, and eventually always finds its way back to the government — somehow or other. . . . .

6 You can have whatever you like, as long as you pay for it. . . . .

7 You run a small company and find some of your workers sitting round chatting. What might you say? 'Come on. . . . .'

8 Someone who doesn't seem to have a lot of sense never seems to be able to keep much money. . . . .

---

* The Treasury: a British government department responsible for public revenue and expenditure.

Writing

Join with 'although'.

Join with 'when'.

Join with 'so … that' and replace 'soon'.

Replace 'then' and make one sentence.
Replace 'soon' and join ideas.

Join with 'and', and replace 'soon'.

Replace 'after a period'.

D The story below is a draft for a magazine, but the editor wants it rewritten. Rewrite it on a separate piece of paper, doing what the editor wants, and using phrases from the box below to replace 'soon', 'then', etc.

FROM RAGS TO RICHES — IN TWELVE MONTHS!

Jane Rich is a millionairess now. She hasn't always had money. / A year ago she had been out of work for three years. She was suddenly offered an office cleaning job. / She took it.

She did the job well. <u>Soon</u> she was being asked to clean offices for other firms. /

<u>Then</u> she started to employ cleaners to work for her. She opened an office. She bought two vans. / <u>Soon</u> the work was coming in fast. She had to employ more people and buy more vans. /

Her accountant advised her to invest her profits in shares. <u>Soon</u> she had doubled her investment. /

<u>After a period</u> she made her first million and bought the firm that had first employed her as a cleaner.

- *later, after a while, in due course* — to replace 'then'
- *in no time at all, in next to no time, before she knew it* — to replace 'soon'
- *finally, in the end, eventually* — to replace 'after a period'

Style and register

E Here are some examples of non-standard English. You might hear English speakers say these things, although educated people do not consider them 'good style'. On a separate piece of paper, write how you would say the same things in more standard English.

0 'We don't hardly go nowhere these days.'
   We hardly go anywhere these days.
1 'She don't spend nothing on her kids.'
2 'I ain't gonna do nothing about it.'
3 'It's the rich what gets the pleasure, and the poor what gets the blame.'
4 'If he'd have worked harder, he'd have done better for hisself.'

A rare and exceptional gift

Grammar

A Which of the listed words and phrases can fill the gaps in the sentences? Circle those that can.

0 This is . . . . the best dinner I've had this year.

   (**a** easily)   **b** easy   **c** rather   **d** far   (**e** by far)   **f** fairly
   (**g** quite) (**h** nowhere near)

1 I feel . . . . better than I did.

   a quite   **b** considerably   **c** more   **d** much   **e** rather   **f** fairly
   g a lot   **h** far

2 It's . . . . as popular as it used to be.

   a nowhere near   **b** not nearly   **c** not quite   **d** by far not
   e nothing like   **f** rather not   **g** just   **h** by no means

3 It was better than . . . .

   a expected   **b** I'd expected   **c** I'd expected it
   d I'd expected it to   **e** I'd expected it to be   **f** before
   g it might have   **h** it might have been

4 We spent more than . . . .

   a meant   **b** we meant   **c** we meant to   **d** we should have
   e we should have done   **f** was sensible   **g** it was sensible
   h it was sensible to   **i** we said we would

B In the text below some of the lines have an extra, unwanted word. Circle it and write it in the space on the right. Tick the space if the line is correct as it stands.

(The) most parents are more than happy if their child is healthy	0 ...*The*...
and contented. But what about those who want a higher	0 ...✓...
achiever? Is there anything they can do to increase the speed of the	1 ....
child's development faster? Certainly there is, but some experts	2 ....
nowadays are saying that genetics play a by far bigger role than	3 ....
thirty years ago it was thought to be the case and parental behaviour	4 ....
is considered much less influential than previously. It was more	5 ....
common than before to play up the importance of nurture, but	6 ....
opinions change. Sociologists have begun to point to the	7 ....
fact that more and the more successful people these days have	8 ....
come from broken homes or, often, children's homes or state care.	9 ....
Nature or nurture? What is the most surprising is that, after all	10 ....
the research, nobody knows the answer. Is this another case of 'the	11 ....
more we learn about something, the less than we know about it'?	12 ....

Vocabulary

C In each case three of the four adverbs given will go comfortably into the sentence. One won't. Circle the odd one out.

0 He was . . . . injured.

   a seriously   **b** slightly   (**c** totally)   **d** badly

1 They were . . . . disappointed.

   a extremely   **b** strongly   **c** bitterly   **d** clearly

2 The . . . . handicapped deserve our understanding more than sympathy.

   a physically   **b** heavily   **c** severely   **d** mentally

3 I'm . . . . lost.

   a completely   **b** hopelessly   **c** totally

   d exceptionally

4 They are . . . . needed.

   a well   **b** badly   **c** urgently   **d** desperately

5 She was . . . . ignorant.

   a blissfully   **b** totally   **c** rather   **d** joyfully

6 You're . . . . right.

   a absolutely   **b** quite   **c** fully   **d** obviously

D Fill in the missing lines in the chain, choosing from the words in the boxes.

fully insured

fully **dressed**

suitably dressed

suitably **impressed**

extremely impressed

extremely **enthusiastic**

wildly enthusiastic

. . . .

. . . .

. . . .

. . . .

. . . .

. . . .

strongly criticised

. . . .

. . . .

. . . .

. . . .

. . . .

. . . .

seriously hurt

easily
absolutely
brutally
heartily
seriously
over-
strongly
highly
thoroughly
terminally
harshly

. . . .

. . . .

. . . .

. . . .

. . . .

. . . .

. . . .

ABSOLUTELY EXHAUSTED!

punished
optimistic
disgusted
criticised
recommended
exhausted
fed-up
ill
sick
hurt
beaten
rated

Reading

E Below are the beginnings of twelve sentences about two child prodigies followed by the second half of the sentences. Match the letters to the numbers to make complete sentences.

0 **Monica Seles**,
ladies tennis champion,
was born in Novi Sad,
where …   ….*I*.

1 Her father, Karolj, was
the sort of father
who …   ……

2 His tactics failed with his
son, Monica's elder
brother, who … ……

3 She won two major European championships
between 1982 and 1985, when …   ……

4 In 1985 they moved to Florida, where …   ……

5 She started playing the international circuit in 1987,
since when …   ……

6 **Ruth Lawrence**
was born in Brighton,
which …   ……

7 She had a father for
whom …   ……

8 At the age of 9 she
passed her 'O' level
examinations,
which …   ……

9 She passed her mathematics 'A' level one year later,
when …   ……

10 At 11 she was awarded a scholarship to Oxford
University, where …   ……

11 On obtaining her degree Ruth took up a fellowship
at Harvard University, which …   ……

A … meant both her and her father moving to the
USA.

B … she was just 10.

C … is a town on the south coast of England.

D … three years later she gained a first-class honours
degree in maths and physics.

E … she has beaten Graf, Navratilova and Sabatini
many times.

F … most pupils sit five or six years later.

G … was too rebellious for the international tennis
circuit.

H … success for his daughter was an all-consuming
preoccupation.

I ✓ … she spent the first twelve years of her life.

J … would stop at nothing to make his child
successful.

K … she was voted Yugoslavian Sportswoman of the
Year.

L … they have lived ever since.

Writing

F Look at these notes about another child prodigy. Write similar sentences to the ones above, using *who(m)*, *whose*, *which*, *where* and *when* to connect information.

- Michael Adams

- b. Truro, Cornwall (south-west England)
  1972 (same year Bobby Fischer became
  world champion)

- normal childhood until 7 — then started
  playing chess

- father quite a good player — taught him
  basics

- age 11, county champion (first time
  someone so young)

- joint winner of under-21 national
  championship (only 14) in 1986

- 1989 — Britain's youngest-ever
  grandmaster (only two other players ever
  qualified at a younger age — Kasparov and
  Fischer, both world champions)

G Make notes on the landmarks, important people, events and places in your own life so far, and then write a short piece connecting the information as you did in **F**.

1C Relative values

Grammar

A What is the difference in meaning between the pairs of sentences below? Write your explanations on a separate piece of paper.

0a James lived with his cousin for five years.

0b James has lived with his cousin for five years.

0a *James no longer lives with his cousin but did so for five years some time in the past.*

0b *James moved in five years ago and is still living there now.*

1a I was staying with my aunt when my uncle died.

1b I stayed with my aunt when my uncle died.

2a This time next week I shall be leaving school for the last time.

2b This time next week I shall have left school for the last time.

3a I left school when I found a job.

3b I had left school when I found a job.

4a Robert helps his grandparents on Saturday.

4b Robert is helping his grandparents on Saturday.

5a Sandra has been working in Hong Kong for a long time.

5b Sandra worked in Hong Kong for a long time.

6a Every morning when I wake up I turn off the alarm clock.

6b Every morning when I wake up I've turned off the alarm clock.

7a When I saw her yesterday, she was crying.

7b When I saw her yesterday, she had been crying.

B Choose one of these verbs to fill the gaps in the text. Put each in the best tense form.

be	catch	come	complete	arrive ✓	do	feel
give	get	have	long	remember	see	start
think (x2)	work					

Dear Paul,

Thanks for your letter which (0) .. *arrived* ..... yesterday morning. I (1) ....
really hard since we last (2) .... each other. Perhaps you (3) .... that I
(4) .... (just) work on an advertising project. By the end of this week I
(5) .... that project and so next week I (6) .... a holiday. I (7) ....
of coming to visit you. How (8) .... (you) about that? Last time I (9) ....,
I (10) .... a train straight after work and (11) .... to your place at ten.
(12) .... (I) that next Friday? Let me know if it (13) .... (not) convenient.
I (14) .... to see you and to hear all your news. I (15) .... you a ring
tomorrow evening to see what you (16) ....

Vocabulary

C In these sentences one half of a pair of words is missing. Which word fills each gap?

0 I've got to write an essay on the . . . *pros* . . . . . and cons of belonging to a large family.

1 Any marriage inevitably has its . . . . and downs.

2 When you first start work, you have to learn to take the rough with the . . . .

3 Falling in love is . . . . and parcel of growing up.

4 We must try and sort out the problem . . . . and for all.

5 'Where have you been?' 'Oh, just here and . . . .'

6 'And what have you been doing?' 'Oh, just . . . . and that.'

7 I've told you time and . . . . not to speak to me like that.

8 It can sometimes be hard to like your own flesh and . . . .

9 I don't understand all the ins and . . . . of their problems.

10 We don't see each other all that often, but we meet every . . . . and then.

D In the text below there are a number of mistakes with phrasal verbs. The wrong preposition or particle has been used. Underline the wrong word(s) and write the correct one(s) in the space on the right.

Sam and I were brought <u>out</u> next door to each other and I always	. . . *up* . . . .
looked over to him as he was a couple of years older than I was.	. . . .
When I was little, he never minded being asked to look at me if my	. . . .
mum had to go out. As I grew in, it seemed only natural that he	. . . .
should take me out to the cinema or to a disco sometimes. We got on	. . . .
well with each other and by the time I left school I had fallen through	. . . .
him in a big way. We went out with each other for a couple of years	. . . .
but then he took a job in Washington and we began to grow out. He	. . . .
suggested I moved to Washington too, which I did, but I found it	. . . .
hard to get through with his smart new friends from work. I hadn't	. . . .
had much of an education and I think he felt that I let him out. We	. . . .
found it impossible to talk over our problems calmly and in the end	. . . .
we split off. I look down on our happier times together with great	. . . .
pleasure and sometimes wonder what would have happened if we	. . . .
hadn't broken down. Mind you, I wouldn't have married Bill then,	. . . .
of course.	

Reading

E In the text below four sentences are in the wrong position. Which are they and where should they be? Write the correct order of sentences (1–14) below.

TWINS

[1] Mary in London suddenly felt sharp pains in her stomach. [2] The pains quickly passed but she knew she had to phone her twin sister, Sue, who was living in New Zealand. [3] Sue's husband told Mary that Sue had just been rushed into hospital with appendicitis. [4] Something rather similar happened with John and Paul. [5] They had been living and teaching at opposite ends of the country for five years but had both just got engaged and so made plans to meet and get to know each other's fiancées. [6] There are frequently newspaper reports about extraordinary coincidences concerning twins. [7] Some of these are about twins who are leading separate adult lives but experience things at exactly the same time as their twin. [8] Other even stranger coincidences concern twins who have been brought up separately, never knowing each other. [9] Anne and Lucy were adopted by different parents immediately after their birth. [10] Anne's new parents took her to Scotland while Lucy stayed in Manchester. [11] When they were thirty the two girls traced each other. [12] All four were amazed to discover that the two girls not only looked like sisters but had identical jobs in banks. [13] To cap it all, when they first met, they were wearing identical red dresses. [14] Not only did the sisters discover that they had each studied foreign languages at university but they also found that they had each had a daughter called Kim born in the same week in 1990.

Correct sentence order: *6,* ....

....

Writing

F These notes about the life of Elizabeth Taylor are taken from a reference book. Write them out in complete sentences on a separate piece of paper.

---

0 Elizabeth Taylor, American film star, born London 1932.
   Elizabeth Taylor, the American film star, was born in London in 1932.

1 moved to Los Angeles 1939, screen debut, age 10, *There's One Born Every Minute*

2 child star, number of films (2 Lassie ones, *Little Women,* etc.)

3 first marriage Nick Hilton, hotelier family, 1950

4 1950s, *Cat on a Hot Tin Roof, Suddenly Last Summer,* Oscar nominations.

5 married 8 times, 2 x Richard Burton, Welsh actor, in *Who's Afraid of Virginia Woolf* together.

6 in life, famous — many things — beauty, acting, alcoholism, AIDS campaigning.

Progress Test 2 (Units 6–10)

SECTION A: WRITING

Time: 45 minutes

You recently attended a meeting at which university and college students talked about their experience of trying to get by on a small amount of money. You made some notes (below), and found out exactly what one student, Carla, spends. Her budget is fairly typical.

Using your notes and the facts about Carla's spending, write a piece for a student magazine suggesting ways that students might manage their budget. You should write about 200 words.

Write your answer on a separate piece of paper.

Carla's total annual income

(Grant	
+ parents' contribution	
+ part-time earnings):	£3,100

Where the money goes

Accommodation (rented room in shared house)	£1,350
Food and housekeeping	£900
Electricity, water and telephone	£150
Travel:	
daily to and from university, and social travel	£50
to and from home town to university	£90
Books and stationery	£120
Clothes	£100
Entertainment and miscellaneous expenses	£250
Total annual expenditure:	£3,010

Main problem – making ends meet – esp. first term – books to buy, etc.

Also food and travel – expensive.

Accommodation and housekeeping – major costs.

Never enough money to buy new clothes.

Might need to get bank loan – esp. towards end of year 1.

Various solutions put forward by students – all to save money:

– Don't eat in college cafés, restaurants. Make your own lunch.

– Buy food, personal items and household necessities in bulk.

– Use (or get) a bike. You could save up to £5 a week on travel.

– Live in or close to university/college. Reduce amount of travel.

– Get student travel reduction (rail / bus) + look for student discounts in shops, hair salons, clubs, sports centres, etc.

– Buy second-hand books and clothes.

– Use hot water and heating only when necessary.

SECTION B: READING

Suggested time: 15 minutes

Read this article. Which of the options printed under the text fit into the gaps? Write the letters in the spaces, as in the example. One of the options will not fit.

FEBRUARY 1993

Major discovery of (headless) dinosaur — 'new' to science

The new dinosaur

The Isle of Wight, off the coast of southern England, is once again the location of one of the greatest archaeological finds of this century.

The Isle of Wight rock formation, known as the Wealden series, (0)..*f*... and has always attracted geologists and fossil-hunters. It is also where, a few years ago, an iguanodon, (1)......, was unearthed.

A year ago this month, another dinosaur was unearthed, this one as large as — but much more complete than — any before, and possibly of a new type. The geologists who discovered the dinosaur remains kept the find secret for ten months (2).......

So far about 100 bones have been found in perfect condition, but they need to be carefully preserved. That's why they are being removed slowly, cleaned and classified, and then they will be dipped in a nylon solution (3)....... Later the creature will be assembled and put on public display.

The dinosaur, which was about 15 metres long from nose to tip of tail, (4)......, and was a slow-moving vegetarian, a little like a brontosaurus.

Sadly the head is missing, (5)......, along with two teeth from another creature, a megalosaurus, that might well have fed on it. Of course (6)...... might have been carried off by some other creatures, or even washed away.

There has been growing interest in dinosaurs in the past few years and it is hoped that this new dinosaur can be exhibited on the island. Because (7)......, the Isle of Wight council is already considering plans to invest £1.6 million in a new 10,000 square foot museum — (8)...... — in the hope of attracting thousands of visitors a year in the future.

a   but most of the rest of the skeleton is there
b   is believed to be some 120 million years old
c   for fear of fossil-hunters plundering the site
d   the present museum in Sandown is far too small
e   while geologists dread the thought

f✓ is famous for its fossils
g   provisionally called Dinosaur Island
h   to prevent them from crumbling
i   the head itself
j   which is now on show in the British Museum

ANSWER KEY

Unit 1 It's a small world

A 1 1 often go abroad on business. 2 ✓. 3 Our car is always breaking down. 4 ✓. 5 ✓. 6 As a young girl I would often read travel books.

B 1 behave, 2 living, 3 working, 4 do, 5 running, 6 feel, 7 having, 8 be

C Possible collocations:

1 a thick / slight / pronounced accent, 2 the space / arms / rat race; 3 to exploit / waste / develop / save water resources, 4 to lose / put on weight, 5 to put forward a proposal / plan / suggestion, 6 a well / badly / college trained employee

D 1 f, 2 k, 3 i, 4 h, 5 b, 6 l, 7 a, 8 g.

E 1 Formal, notice out of doors; (vocabulary — trespassers, prosecuted)

2 Informal, conversation; (idiom — couldn't believe my eyes —, rather long and loosely structured sentence) or a letter to a friend

3 Formal, travel brochure (vocabulary — aquamarine, abundant, spectacular, fringed)

4 Formal, written, brochure of an international investment company (vocabulary — offer clients invaluable advice and assistance)

F 1 Please do not smoke in bed. 2 You can have dinner in your own room for a small extra charge. 3 If you need an early morning call, could you please ask reception before 10 o'clock on the previous evening. 4 We suggest that you ask our reception staff to put any valuables in the hotel safe for you.

Unit 2 What's in a word?

A 1 b, c, d, 2 a, c, e, 3 b, 4 d.

B 1 You should have trained harder.
(Then) you could have run faster.
You might have won the race.
(And then) you would have got the gold medal.

2 You shouldn't have stolen the money.
You could have borrowed it.

You might have been able to borrow it from me.
(And then) you wouldn't have got into trouble.

3 You shouldn't have bought a new car.
You could have bought a second-hand one.
It might have been just as reliable.
You would have saved a lot of money.

4 You shouldn't have given up the piano.
You could have become a really good player.
You might have been good enough to turn professional.
You would have earned more than you do as a teacher.

C 1 I wish English didn't have so many words...

2 I wish I had concentrated more in...

3 I wish I could imitate English...

4 I wish I was lazing on the beach (and) not sitting...

5 I wish somebody would explain to me the...

6 I wish there were clearer rules...

D 1 widely spoken, 2 substantial percentage, 3 logical connection, 4 grammatical association, 5 effective learning, 6 absolutely ridiculous.

E 1 B: I'm not bad at history.
A: What are you really bad at?
B : Well, I'm a bit hopeless at maths.
A: What particular problems do you have with maths?
B: I never seem to have enough time, so I don't normally manage to finish the work. I can just about cope with simple sums but I just don't/ can't get the point of algebra.
A: I think you could do with being more confident.

2 B: I think I have a certain aptitude for history.
A: What are your weaknesses?
B: I have no real flair for mathematics.
A: What difficulties do you experience with mathematics?
B: I always find I have insufficient time, and for this reason I rarely succeed in completing (the) assignments. I am normally able to handle basic arithmetic; however, I fail to see the point of most algebraic equations.
A: I feel you suffer/are suffering from a lack of confidence.

F 1 I should/would be (very/most) grateful if you would/ could send me your latest catalogue and price lists.

2 It would be of great help if you could let us have further details.

3 I would really appreciate it if you could/would let me know by/before the end of this week.

4 Could we ask you to fax (the) information (through to us) as soon as possible?

5 I wonder if/whether it would/might be possible for you to inform us of your decision in the very near future.

6 Perhaps you would be kind enough to provide us with (the) exact numbers by Friday at the (very) latest.

G 1 1 c, 2 h, 3 e, 4 b, 5 f, 6 d, 7 a

2 for all = b, odd = b, broad = a, disguise = a, cultivate = b, practice = b, top schools = a, perfect = b.

Unit 3 It's a fact!

A 1 all possible; 2 a, b, c, f, g; 3 a, b, e, f, g; 4 b, c, d, g; 5 b, e.

B 1 had never played, 2 dreamed/dreamt/thought, 3 had been suffering, 4 was standing/was waiting, 5 felt/could feel, 6 knocking/trembling/shaking/collapse/give way, 7 called/shouted/said/yelled/whispered/announced, 8 sat/ knelt/bent, 9 took/pulled, 10 put/pulled, 11 was standing/ was getting, 12 breathing/sighing, 13 went, 14 had arrived/come, 15 had no sooner taken, 16 found, 17 lying, 18 had tied, 19 lay, 20 listened, 21 laughing/ laugh, 22 had never felt/had never been/have never felt/ have never been, 23 believe, 24 is/was, 25 began/started/ took off.

C 1 B: he must have been running.
   C: He might have been pushing his car.
2 B: the baby must have been crying all night.
   C: He might have had some bad news.
3 B: he must have been drinking last night.
   C: He might have caught a cold
4 B: he must have cut himself shaving.
   C: He might have been fighting/might have had a fight with someone.

D This is a sample rewritten version:

You may have seen and anyway you must have heard of 'Citizen Kane', the classic film made by Orson Welles at the age of 25. It was the story of a multi-millionaire whose life was one of extreme luxury but who failed to find happiness.

Not only did Welles direct the film, he also wrote the script and starred in it. When the film was first shown, in 1941, it was considered by all the critics to be a truly remarkable achievement for such a young man.

Even today, amazingly enough, according to many experts it is the best film ever made and 50 years later it is still regularly (being) shown in cinemas around the world.

E This is the most likely grouping, but some variation may be possible.

Money/Finance	Jobs
reward	warden
lease	contractor
receipt	psychiatrist
deposit	clerk
debt	porter

Marriage	Animals/Creatures
bride	goat
witness	beetle
widow	cattle
groom	caterpillar
registrar	butterfly

F 1 B, 2 D, 3 J, 4 G, 5 K, 6 H, 7 I, 8 A, 9 C, 10 F.

Unit 4 News of the world

A 1 c, 2 b, 3 b, 4 c, 5 a, 6 c, 7 d, 8 b.

B Here are just a few examples:
1 suspect: prep. 'of', (a) suspicion, a suspect (b) suspicious. 2 compliment: prep. 'on', (a) compliment, (b) complimentary. 3 insist: prep. 'on', (a) insistence, (b) insistent. 4 argue: prep 'about'/'with', (a) argument, (b) argumentative. 5 stress: No prep. (a) stress, (b) stressful. 6 regret: No prep. (a) regret, (b) regretful, regrettable, 7 establish: No prep. (a) establishment, (b) established. 8 allege: No prep. (a) allegation, (b) alleged. 9 agree: 'with' someone/'with'/'to' an idea. (a) agreement, (b) agreeable/disagreeable. 10 believe: believe someone (No prep.)/believe in something. (a) belief, (b) believable/unbelievable.

C 1 Robert Lynd felt that people welcomed almost any break in the monotony of things, and added that a man had only to murder a series of wives in a new way to become known to millions of people who had never heard of Homer.

2 John Bogart admitted that when a dog bit a man that was not news but when a man bit a dog, that was news.

3 Charles Dickens insisted that newspapers were so filthy and bestial that no honest man would admit one into his house for a water closet doormat.

4 John Osborne warned people never to believe in mirrors or newspapers.

5 Lord Thomson declared that it was part of the social mission of every great newspaper to provide a refuge and a home for the largest possible number of salaried eccentrics.

6 G. K. Chesterton pointed out that journalism consisted largely of saying "Lord Jones dead" to people who had never known he was alive / who didn't know that he had been alive.

7 Irving Rabbit wrote that the American reading his Sunday paper in a state of lazy collapse was perhaps the most perfect symbol of the triumph of quantity over quality and added that whole forests were being ground into pulp to minister to their triviality.

D 1 … to have been in prison several times. 2 … writing / (that) we wrote / (that) we write / (that) we should write to the editor. 3 … to reconsider his decision. 4 … to be planning a new film version of Robin Hood. 5 … to being criticised by non-professionals. 6 … on conducting a marvellous interview. 7 … to be a millionaire. 8 … to have killed her husband.

E 1 Very important information about possible changes in the boardroom became known yesterday. 2 Twenty British people were/have been forced to leave Uclesia as a result of a diplomatic argument. 3 The President (yesterday) promised to limit government spending yesterday. 4 The/Our local football team was easily beaten in the/their match last night. 5 The government was strongly criticised yesterday as the number of unemployed people was announced to be higher than it had ever been before. 6 Share prices fell steeply yesterday after secret information from the Finance Ministry was published.

F 1 The British government set up the World Service as the international voice of Britain overseas with the aim of binding the Empire together. 2 Its aims have changed every decade moving from the desire in the 30s to bind the Empire, to the anti-fascist propaganda of the 40s, to the aims of fighting the Cold War in the 50s through to serving the goal of de-colonisation in the 60s. 3 The World Service today broadcasts in 36 languages and to almost every part of the world. 4 It broadcasts a variety of programmes dealing with news, sport, art, religion and science. (or … a variety of programmes from news, sport and art to religion and science.) 5 It receives frequent requests to start broadcasting in more languages such as Sinhala.

Unit 5 Out of this world

A 1 He sounded very apologetic yesterday. He sounded just like his father. 2 She looked so pale when she arrived. She looked as if/as though she had seen a ghost. 3 This new perfume smells dreadful. It smells like old socks! 4 You sound worried. You sound as if/as though you have had some bad news. 5 After the operation, I felt quite ill. I felt as if/as though I had been hit by a lorry! 6 The soup tastes/tasted awful! It tastes/tasted like soap, not soup! 7 The coffee they gave us smelled/smelt fine, but it tasted as if/as though it had been made last week.

B 1 to have been wandering, 2 to have been blown out, 3 to be getting/to have got, 4 to come/to be coming, 5 to have lost.

C 1 Mice/teeth, 2 analyses/criteria, 3 Lice/children, 4 aircraft/phenomena, 5 spacecraft.

D 1 shockproof, 2 waterproof, 3 homesick, 4 childproof, 5 airtight.

E Possible version:
I get very annoyed with my parents because they are always criticising everything I do. Yesterday my father threatened to throw out all my cassettes if I didn't tidy up my room. And then he just stood there staring while I worked for ages putting things away into drawers and onto shelves. It really irritated me, especially since, instead of helping, he repeatedly criticised my friends for calling to see me at any time and me for talking to them on the phone for ages.

F phenomena 3, site 5, threshold 8, spacecraft 6, mystified 1, product 4, extra-terrestrial 7, investigation 2. ('analysis' and 'edge' do not fit.)

G 1 b, 2 d, 3 a, 4 d, 5 b

H Here is a sample letter to the newspaper:
Sir,
I refer to the article on 'Crop circles' that appeared in yesterday's edition of your newspaper. Personally, I can't believe in the extra-terrestrial theory. I think many of the marks might have been made by cows or some other animals. And from other photos I have seen, most of them certainly look as if they have been made by people. I must say, though, that it's strange none of the 'hoaxers' have been caught yet!
Yours sincerely,

PROGRESS TEST 1 (Units 1–5)

A This is a sample of the kind of letter you should aim to write here:

Dear Tom, Dick and Harry,

Hope you're all well and still keen on the idea of a holiday together in the spring. Remember we thought that North Wales could be a good spot? Well, I saw an ad from UK Country Homes which has several places on offer in Wales.

I thought I'd ring them up and find out a bit more before getting in touch with you all. They tell me they have several cottages in the Snowdonia area of North Wales and their prices are very reasonable at only £125 each for two weeks. Two weeks, by the way, is the minimum booking. What makes it sound even more attractive is that the £125 includes the cost of a hired car as well as linen, gas and electricity!

They told me on the phone that we'd have to book as soon as possible as Wales is a really popular destination. What do you think? We only have to pay a £10 deposit each and I'd be happy to do that. How about the first two weeks in May? That would suit me perfectly. I've sent for brochures and have asked them to send you all copies too.

Do let me know as soon as possible whether I should go ahead and make a booking.

All the best,   [214 words]

B 1 G, 2 E, 3 F, 4 A, 5 C. (Suggestions B and D do not apply.)

C1 1 Here it's rare for people to go shopping on Sundays. 2 My father would always take me fishing with him. 3 She can't get used to studying every evening. 4 I wish I had paid more attention to the lecture. 5 On hearing the news, she broke down. 6 I might have got a better job if I had studied harder. 7 Strange as/though it may seem, I've never wanted to go to America. 8 She seems to be having a good time. 9 You must have been holding the thing upside down. 10 She's known to be living in France.

C2 1 <u>had died</u> = died, 2 <u>was</u> = had been, 3 <u>suffered</u> = had been suffering, 4 ✓, 5 <u>has danced</u> = had danced, 6 <u>was retiring</u> = retired, 7 <u>must</u> = had to, 8 ✓, 9 <u>has been</u> = was, 10 ✓

C3 1 When he admitted that he had been listening to her on the phone and (that he) had heard everything, she accused him of being a hypocrite, but/and then apologised for what she had done earlier.

2 After she had implored them to think it over again and promised that she would, they agreed (to do the same), but warned her not to expect too much.

3 When he reminded her that they had to leave by six and suggested that they could (in fact) leave earlier, she confessed (that) she had forgotten the concert was tonight/that night, and then demanded to know how she could possibly be ready that early.

C4 1 taken or expressed, 2 reached or made, 3 put or place, 4 make, 5 desire or wish, 6 cause or give, 7 convinced or positive or certain, 8 flair or talent, 9 considerably or far or much, 10 succeeded.

Progress Test 1: Scoring Scheme

To mark and score the Progress Test, we suggest this simple scoring scheme: Maximum

A	An impression mark (0–5) for each of these criteria:	
	● Task achievement — (the sample contains the points that should be made)	max. 10
	● Organisation —	max. 10
	● Range of language employed (structure and vocabulary) —	max. 10
	● Accuracy of language —	max. 10
	Total possible maximum for **A**	40
B	5 'items' x 4 points each	20
C 1	10 items x 2 points each	20
2	10 items x 1 point each	10
3	3 items x 5 points each	15
4	10 items x 1 point each	10
	Total possible maximum for **C**	55

Unit 6   We're all in the same boat

A 1b The thing we need for this project is global support.

1c What is needed for this project is global support.

2b If something had been done earlier, the situation would not have deteriorated.

2c Had something had been done earlier, the situation would not have deteriorated.

3b If we were to ban/were to have a ban on hunting, most people would approve.

3c Were there (to be) a ban on hunting, most people would approve.

4b This should have been taken into consideration 20 years ago.

4c Someone ought to have taken this into consideration 20 years ago.

5b It's about time we showed these animals a little more respect.

5c It's high time these animals were shown a little more respect.

6b The problem could probably have been solved before it became so serious.

6c We might have been able to solve the problem before it became so serious.

7b What is tragic is that millions of birds are dying unnecessarily.

7c The fact that millions of birds are dying unnecessarily is tragic.

8b What we might be faced with is famine on a massive scale.

8c Famine on a massive scale is what we might be faced with.

B 1 F, 2 D, 3 K, 4 H, 5 A, 6 B, 7 C, 8 L, 9 E, 10 I, 11 G.

C 1 C, 2 G, 3 H, 4 I, 5 B, 6 A, 7 J, 8 E, 9 D.

D 1 L, 2 F, 3 B, 4 P, 5 J, 6 D, 7 G, 8 A, 9 S, 10 E, 11 H, 12 R, 13 C, 14 M, 15 N, 16 T, 17 K, 18 O

E What the poem says is that we humans are stupid (dumb, deaf and blind). In fact, in spite of our intelligence and achievements, we smile at what we have done and are doing to the planet, and are more stupid than any other creatures that live or have ever lived on earth.

F This is a sample of the kind of article you should aim to write:
People were still numbed today, twenty-four hours after the tanker carrying 40,000 tons of crude oil ran aground on the shore of a small Canadian island. Many residents were too shocked and bewildered to speak, but one told me that the air was horrible and full of pollution. He added that one read about such things happening, but never dreamed it could happen on one's own doorstep.

As helicopters sprayed chemicals on the vast area of oil on the water, a member of an environmental group complained that these chemicals would do as much if not more damage than the oil itself. She maintained that

dispersal of the oil should be done by mechanical means, not chemical.

A government spokesman on the spot promised that they would be holding a full enquiry and that no stone would be left unturned in an attempt to discover the cause of the accident. Meanwhile an island farmer affirmed that he would be seeking compensation, not just for what had happened to his animals but for what might have happened: things that no one would know for years to come.

A Canadian ornithologist commented sadly that the loss to wildlife of all kinds, birds, fish and animals, was incalculable. He thought the tragic death toll might run to millions.

When asked for his version of events, the tanker's captain declined to comment.

Unit 7   Just a phase they're going through

A The correct order of the sentences: **c** 1, **h** 2, **i** 3, **a** 4, **g** 5, **f** 6, **d** 7, **b** 8.

B This is an example of the kind of letter you should aim to write:
Dear —,
Thank you for writing to me. I can understand very well how both you and your parents feel.

My advice would be that you do not drop the idea of going to university. You are fortunate that you have the ability to go and it would be a pity to waste your opportunities. Going on with your studies does not mean you would have to split up with your boyfriend. Indeed, many universities provide hostel accommodation for married couples. It is very likely that, if you return to the idea of going to university, you will be able to bring your parents round to the idea of your marriage.

Studying further may mean that you and your boyfriend will have less money now but it should ensure that you get more interesting and better-paid jobs later.

I do wish you all the best for your future.
Yours sincerely,
Halina Swift   [150 words]

C   **(a) Nouns** — rash, mumps, bully, tease, mop, day-dreamer, poster, cheat, common, glance, squint, sigh, tingle, kid, teenager, nurse

  (b) Verbs — bully, tease, mock, mop, blush, cheat, confiscate, glance, squint, sigh, tingle, kid, nurse

  (c) Adjectives — rebellious, rash, heartbroken, unsightly, self-conscious, common, clumsy, cautious

D I mop, 2 confiscated, 3 rash, 4 bully, 5 glanced,
6 poster, sighing, 7 squint, 8 clumsy

E Open-ended.

F 1 I now wish I hadn't turned down the job.
2 I don't regret telling him he was a bully.
3 I'll always remember meeting him for the first time.
4 I regret being/having been so rebellious as a teenager.
5 I wish my father had told me more about his childhood.

G remember once not to do > remember once not doing, instead of to go > instead of going, for collecting > to collect, listen to > listening to, I had been in > I was in, I had confiscated my Walkman > I had my Walkman confiscated, I was used to be in trouble > I was used to being in trouble, was also made correct > was also made to correct, lucky not being expelled > lucky not to be expelled / not to have been expelled

H Possible sentences:
1 'John's writing is appalling/dreadful!' 2 'John doesn't show the remotest/slightest interest in any of his lessons.' 3 John is a natural leader, but he should take care that his influence is always a positive one. 4 John is a late developer. 5 'John hasn't got a clue about even the simplest maths.' 6 John needs to remember his manners at times.

Unit 8   Rich man, poor man

A 1a The collapse of the company can be traced back to bad management.
or You can trace the collapse of the company back to bad management.
1b The reason why the company collapsed was bad management.
2a Social injustices (can) often have (their) roots in government policies.
2b Government policies can lead to social injustices.
3a The reasons for some people turning to crime are fairly easy to understand.
3b It's fairly easy to understand why some people turn to crime.
4a Social problems often result from unemployment.
4b Unemployment often leads to social problems.

B 1 eXpense, 2 weAlth, 3 sTeal // 4 invEstor, 5 priCeless, 6 ecoNomise, 7 invAluable, 8 esTimate, 9 prIce,

10 poveRty, 11 makE out, 12 ricHes, 13 speNd, 14 profIt
Answer: INHERITANCE TAX

C 1 B, 2 G, 3 C, 4 I, 5 D, 6 H, 7 K, 8 J.

D A sample composition:
Although Jane Rich is a millionairess now, she hasn't always had money. A year ago, she had been out of work for three years when she was suddenly offered an office cleaning job. She took it.
She did the job so well that before she knew it she was being asked to clean offices for other firms.
After a while she started to employ cleaners to work for her, so she opened an office and bought two vans. In next to no time the work was coming in so fast (that) she had to employ more people and buy more vans.
Her accountant advised her to invest her profits in shares and in no time at all she had doubled her investment.
Eventually she made her first million and bought the firm that had first employed her as a cleaner.

E Possible 'standard English' versions:
1 She doesn't spend anything on her children.
2 I'm not going to do anything about it.
3 The rich get the pleasure and the poor get the blame.
or It's the rich who/that get the pleasure and the poor who/that get the blame.
4 If he had worked harder, he would have done better for himself.

Unit 9   A rare and exceptional gift

A 1 b, d, e, g, h, 2 a, b, c, e, g, h, 3 a, b, e, f, h, 4 c, d, e, f, h, i.

B 1 ✓, 2 faster, 3 by, 4 it, 5 ✓, 6 than, 7 ✓, 8 the, 9 ✓, 10 the, 11 ✓, 12 than

C 1 b, 2 b, 3 d, 4 a, 5 d, 6 c

D wildly **optimistic** > **over**-optimistic > over-**rated** > **highly** rated > highly **recommended** > **strongly** recommended > strongly **criticised** > **harshly** criticised > harshly **punished** > **brutally** punished > brutally **beaten** > **easily** beaten > easily **hurt** > **seriously** hurt > seriously **ill** > **terminally** ill > terminally **sick** > **heartily** sick (of) > heartily **fed-up** (with) > **thoroughly** fed-up > thoroughly **disgusted** > **absolutely** disgusted > absolutely **exhausted**!

E 1 J, 2 G, 3 K, 4 L, 5 E, 6 C, 7 H, 8 F, 9 B, 10 D, 11 A

F This is a sample of what you should aim to write:
Michael Adams comes from Truro, Cornwall, in the south-west of England. He was born in 1972, which was the same year in which Bobby Fischer became world chess champion. He had a normal childhood until the age of seven, when he started playing chess. His father, who was quite a good player himself, taught him the basics of the game. When he was 11, he became county champion, which was the first time anyone so young had done this. In 1986, when he was still only 14, he was the joint winner of the under-21 national championship. In 1989 he became Britain's youngest-ever grandmaster; only two other players have ever qualified at younger ages — Kasparov and Fischer — both of whom went on to become world champions.

G Open-ended

Unit 10   Relative values

A   1a The speaker was with her aunt at the time of her uncle's death.

   1b She went to stay with her aunt after her uncle's death.

   2a The person will be in the process of leaving school in one week's time.

   2b The speaker is leaving school some time in the next six days.

   3a The speaker first found a job and then left school.

   3b He or she first left school and later found a job.

   4a Robert is in the habit of helping his grandparents every Saturday.

   4b Robert will be helping his grandparents this coming Saturday.

   5a Sandra started working in Hong Kong a long time ago and is still working there.

   5b Sandra worked in Hong Kong for a long period in the past, but doesn't work there any longer.

   6a Every morning the speaker wakes up and then turns off the alarm clock.

   6b Every morning the speaker somehow manages to turn off the alarm clock before he or she wakes up.

   7a The speaker actually saw the tears falling down the other person's cheeks.

   7b The speaker didn't actually see the person crying but realised that she had just/recently stopped crying.

B 1 have been working, 2 saw, 3 remember, 4 had just started/was just starting, 5 will/shall have completed, 6 am having/will be having/am going to have, 7 was thinking/had thought/am thinking, 8 would you feel/do you feel, 9 came, 10 caught, 11 got, 12 Shall I do/Could I do, 13 is not, 14 am longing, 15 will give, 16 think.

C 1 ups, 2 smooth, 3 part, 4 once, 5 there, 6 this, 7 again, 8 blood, 9 outs, 10 now

D (1) looked <u>over</u> > up, (2) look <u>at</u> > after, (3) grow <u>in</u> > up, (4) fallen <u>through</u> > for, (5) grow <u>out</u> > apart, (6) get <u>through with</u> > on with, (7) let him <u>out</u> > down, (8) split <u>off</u> > up, (9) look <u>down on</u> > back on, (10) broken <u>down</u> > up.

E Correct sentence order: 6, 7, 1, 2, 3, 4, 5, 12, 8, 9, 10, 11, 14, 13.

F Possible version:
   1   Having moved to Los Angeles in 1939, she made her screen debut at the age of 10 in *There's One Born Every Minute*.

   2   As a child star she made a number of films including two Lassie ones and *Little Women*.

   3   Her first marriage was to Nick Hilton, son of the hotelier family in 1950.

   4   In the 1950s, she starred in *Cat on a Hot Tin Roof* and *Suddenly Last Summer*, for both of which she received Oscar nominations.

   5   She has been married eight times, including twice to Richard Burton, the Welsh actor, with whom she made *Who's Afraid of Virginia Woolf*.

   6   In her life she has been famous for many things— her beauty, her acting, her alcoholism and now her campaigning on behalf of AIDS sufferers.

PROGRESS TEST 2 (Units 6–10)

A This is a sample of the kind of article you should aim to write:

Do you find it hard to make ends meet? For most of us, existing on about £3,000 a year is extremely difficult. The problem is particularly acute in the first term of any year when you have to buy lots of books.

   Carla, a second-year zoology student, is typical. Over two-thirds of her income goes on basic living expenses, leaving only about £500 for travel, books, clothes and entertainment. No wonder she says that she rarely buys any new clothes. She is constantly on the lookout for ways to economise.

So here are some ideas for Carla and others like her. You can't really save much on accommodation costs but you can save on fares by travelling by bike or by living close to the university. You can cut down on living expenses by minimising the amounts of hot water and heating that you use. You can save a great deal by making your own packed lunches rather than eating in the student dining-room.

Buy things in the cheapest possible way: you can, for example, buy food in bulk or get second-hand clothes and books. And don't forget that student discounts are available in lots of local shops as well as for quite a few services.

If you have any other good money-saving tips, do send them in to the Editor. We are planning a full-page feature on economising next month. [233 words]

B 1 j, 2 c, 3 h, 4 b, 5 a, 6 i, 7 d, 8 g.

C1 1 C, 2 B, 3 A, 4 C, 5 D, 6 C, 7 C, 8 A, 9 A, 10 C

C2 1 shut, 2 black, 3 up, 4 fell, 5 up, 6 after, 7 dead, 8 outs, 9 tooth, 10 up, 11 apart, 12 part, 13 upside, 14 miss, 15 stood

C3 1 deeply offended, 2 exceptional talent, 3 awkward silence, 4 physically handicapped, 5 infinitely prettier, 6 hermetically sealed, 7 hopelessly lost, 8 priceless collection, 9 happily married, 10 increasing pressure

C4 Possible version:

… It was bad enough blushing and stammering every time he spoke to Helen, which was the effect she had on him. She had been encouraging him, not only with her eyes, but with her body language, and Ron was very interested in body language. He had even been reading a good book about it, although it hadn't helped him, A schoolmate Bob and his 'crowd', whom he hated, were always making fun of his attempts to persuade Helen to go out with him, but he promised he would show them one day.

At the time he had been trying to learn to play the guitar for some six months, but decided to give it up, as he had realised guitar-playing was not for him. And it was then that he decided to play the keyboard. After only two hours spent in the local music shop, he had decided to save up for a Yamaha. He even thought at the time that the shop might take his guitar as a deposit. He was determined to buy one and promised himself that by the following year he would have joined a pop group.

Progress Test 2: Scoring Scheme

To mark and score the Progress Test, we suggest this simple scoring scheme: Maximum

A	See Progress Test 1	
	Total possible maximum for **A**	40
B	8 'items' × 2 points each	16
C 1	10 items × 1 points each	10
2	15 items × 1 point each	15
3	10 items × 1 points each	10
4	Impression mark	20
	Total possible maximum for **C**	55

Unit 11   All in a day's work

A Matching numbers and letters, with possible sentences:

1g I became a sailor to see the world.

2i I became self-employed so that I didn't/wouldn't have to take orders from others (or so as not to take orders from others).

3f I trained as an artist with a view to being a professional cartoonist.

4c I did a management course in case I (ever) wanted to set up my own management advice bureau.

5d I became a bi-lingual secretary (in order/so as) to use my languages.

6h I originally went into acting so that I might become a film producer.

7a I went into medical research so as to/in order to help cure terrible diseases.

8b I became a professional violinist so that I could play in an orchestra and not teach.

B 1 a, b, c, d, 2 a, b, c, d, 3 d, 4 b, c.

C 1 Have you ever been afraid of being made redundant?

2 Do you intend to stay/staying with the company for a long time?

3 Have you ever fancied/do you ever fancy managing one of our branches abroad?

4 Do you dread being asked to be a courier?

5 Have you any intention of leaving the company in/within the next two years?

Possible further questions:

Do you aim/Are you aiming to make a career with the company?

Do you loathe being asked to do certain jobs (in the office)?

Do you expect to be promoted within the next five years?

Are you ever anxious about losing your job/being moved to a different branch?

D sub-committee, sub-aqua, sub-human; self-employed, self-confident, self-reform; anti-social, anti-freeze, anti-reform, anti-American; co-director, co-educational, co-owner; pro-reform, pro-American; part-time, part-owner, part-human; super-efficient, super-human; high-calibre, high-flier, high-level, high-pitched; low-level, low-pitched, low-level.

E 1 co-owner *or* part-owner, 2 high-pitched, 3 anti-social, 4 sub-committee, 5 high-calibre, super-efficient, high-level, self-employed *or* self-confident.

F 1 The printing mistakes are: (1.39) scarred (from the verb *to scar*) > scared (from the verb *to scare*), (1.53) siting (from the verb *to site* = to place) > sitting (from the verb *to sit*), (1.64) waging (from the verb *to wage*, as in 'to wage war') > wagging (from the verb *to wag* = to shake), (1.66) bared (from the verb *to bare*) > barred (from the verb *to bar*), (1.79) stripped (from the verb *to strip*) > striped (from *stripe*)

2 a) thrilled (1.21) = excited, b) probationary (1.25) = trial (period of time), c) divulge (1.26) = [formal] say, d) substantial (1.32) = here, quite big, e) oust (1.35) = push (the other) out, f) the mechanics of (1.42) = 'the way it works', g) emphatically (1.47) = forcefully, h) petty (1.58) = ridiculously unimportant, i) numerous (1.71) = many

3 a) Not told, b) True, c) False, d) True, e) True

Unit 12 The persuaders

A 1 that, –,–, the, 2 –, –, the, 3 who/that, the, –, 4 that, –, –, –, the, –

B 1 a U, b C, c C, d C, e U, f U/(C), g C/U, h U/(C)
2 a U, b U, c U, d U, e U/(C), f U/C, g C, h C
3 a U, b U, c U, d U(C), e U, f U
4 a U, b C, c U, d U

C 1 B, 2 A, 3 D, 4 D, 5 C, 6 B, 7 A, 8 B, 9 D, 10 A

D Possible answers:
1 short, 2 fat, 3 stale, 4 untalented/mediocre, 5 untidy, 6 too old, 7 strange/weird, 8 poor/uninteresting, 9 dishonest, 10 ugly rubbish bins

E a 4, b 2, c 5, d 10, e 6, f 1, g 3, h 8, i 7, j 9

F 1 creases / wash, 2 reads / work, 3 selling/holding, 4 records/photographs, 5 handles/handled, corners/cornered

G 1 1, 2 C, 3 E, 4 F, 5 J, 6 B, 7 A, 8 D, 9 G

H This is a sample of the kind of letter you should aim to write:

Dear Sir or Madam,

I am writing to express my concern regarding your recent advertising campaign for the 'Carnation' hairspray, shampoo and hair conditioner range and the 'Magic' deodorant and after-shave collection.

I was horrified to discover last week that these products, which you claim to be 'environmentally friendly', are in fact tested on live animals such as mice, rats and even cats. I would like to point out that simply not using CFCs in your aerosols does not qualify you to be termed 'environmentally friendly'. You can, after all, hardly argue that torturing defenceless animals with whom we share this planet is being friendly to the environment.

I have written to the Animal Rights organisation, the local newspaper and my local member of parliament on this matter and enclose copies of these letters. Could I respectfully suggest that you either change your advertising campaign to make it more honest or, preferably, find alternative ways of testing your products?

Yours faithfully,   [158 words]

Unit 13 Travel broadens the mind

A 1 from, 2 through/in, 3 round, 4 round, 5 into, 6 of, 7 on/by/at, 8 to, 9 for, 10 down, 11 up, 12 for, 13 in, 14 at, 15 with/in, 16 on, 17 on/on to, 18 off, 19 for, 20 in, 21 at, 22 by.

B (1) the local residents' traditional lifestyle, (2) the desirability of (3) exotic locations, (4) Recent developments, (5) such holidays are proving increasingly popular, (6) a predominantly rural-based economy,

C Negative: brawling, a drag, to make a quick buck, lout, to shove, shoddy, erosion, bland
Positive: trim, to relish, hospitality, sparkling, picturesque

D 1 hospitality, 2 sparkling, 3 drag, 4 relish, 5 lout, 6 make a quick buck, 7 shoving, 8 bland 9 picturesquely, 10 trim.

E 1 <u>fly</u> > flight, 2 <u>widen</u> > broaden, 3 <u>office</u> > surgery, 4 <u>injury</u> > damage, 5 <u>word</u> > note, 6 <u>fit</u> > agree, 7 <u>sacrifice</u> > victim, 8 <u>brain</u> > mind.

F 1 distance, 2 reach, 3 odds, 4 jungle, 5 recognition/belief, 6 impact/effect/influence.

G This is a sample of the kind of description you should aim to write:

Last summer Jim and Jan went on a week's cycling holiday. They packed panniers for their bikes with all the camping and sports equipment they thought they could possibly need and set off. They spent the first day sightseeing in Jacktown as Jan was particularly keen to visit the art gallery there.

They were quite glad, however, to leave the town behind and head for the hills. It took them the next day to make their way through the spectacular Chean Gorge as Jim kept insisting they stopped to take yet another photograph. They also spent a pleasant couple of hours fishing in the river. They even caught their supper.

They set up camp next day in the Blackway Mountains where they would stay for two nights. One of the highlights of their week was a marvellous walk high in the mountains. As they are both enthusiastic bird-watchers, they were very excited to see eagles soaring above their heads.

They were sorry to leave the mountains but it was time to be getting on their way and they were eager to see something of the sea before returning home. As soon as they reached the coast, however, the weather changed for the worse. They ate a picnic on the beach in the pouring rain, huddled together for warmth.

On the last day of their trip the weather was perfect, however. They rode further along the coast to Banta Bay where they were able to sunbathe and swim to their hearts' content. From Banta Bay it was a short ride home. They got back, tired but happy and already making plans for their next cycle tour. [275 words]

Unit 14   A chapter of accidents

A 1 ... from the national library were saved by policemen.

2 ... will ever be rebuilt.

3 ... are used for disarmament negotiations.

4 ... is slowly being brought under control.

5 ... was hurt in the fire.

6 ... had been led out before the fire could reach them.

B 1 had all been drinking, 2 must have been dreaming, 3 are you doing, 4 was coming, 5 can't be driving (*or possibly* can't have been driving), 6 ought to have been watching, 7 were crossing, 8 should all be playing, 9 will not/shall not/won't/shan't be driving, 10 am not thinking/am not going to think (*or possibly* have not been thinking)

C a chapter of accidents, a crowd of people, a pile of papers, a flock of sheep, a herd of cattle, a pack of wolves, a team of experts, a catalogue of disasters, a bunch of grapes, a chain of shops, a fleet of oil tankers

D 1 a chain of shops, a fleet of oil tankers, 2 a team of experts, 3 a flock of sheep, a herd of cattle, 4 a pile of papers

E This is a sample of the kind of article you should aim to write:
<u>Heavy Floods in [Scotland]</u>
Yesterday evening the east coast of [Scotland] was hit by gales and high tides. Thousands of acres near the coast were flooded and hundreds of people had to be evacuated to higher ground. Rescue centres were opened on hills around the flooded area and many people were taken there for emergency medical care. Among the places which suffered were a number of hotels and holiday homes.

Transport was also badly affected with cars being swept away by the floods. The two main roads into the area are still closed as two bridges have been washed away. Many people were injured in the floods but fortunately only one person has drowned.

Weather conditions are not expected to improve as snow and blizzards are forecast for tomorrow. All possible precautions against further disaster are being taken but visitors and holiday-makers are strongly advised to avoid the area.

F 1 h, 2 c, 3 a, 4 f, 5 b, 6 g.

Unit 15   All work and no play ...

A 1a They nearly managed to win.

1b They nearly succeeded in winning.

1c They just/narrowly failed to win.

1d They were/came very close to winning.

2a It's no use asking him.

2b There's no point in asking him.

2c It's not worth asking him.

or He's not worth asking.

2d It's pointless asking him.

3a It wasn't difficult for me to answer the questions.

or I didn't find it difficult to answer the questions.

or The questions weren't difficult for me to answer.

3b I had no trouble answering the questions.

3c It was easy for me to answer the questions.

or I found it easy to answer the questions.

or The questions were easy for me to answer.

3d I answered/could answer/was able to answer the questions easily.

3e I answered/could answer/was able to answer the questions with ease.

B 1 ever meet/will ever meet/shall ever meet, 2 buy/am buying/am going to buy/I'll buy, 3 have ever eaten, 4 spoke, 5 come, 6 saw, 7 am going to remind/'ll remind/am reminding, 8 have ever been, 9 have ever tried, 10 ever went/had ever been/had ever gone

C 1 D, 2 O, 3 H, 4 I, 5 N, 6 G, 7 F, 8 C, 9 E, 10 A, 11 J, 12 L, 13 P, 14 M, 15 B (Other pairs are possible.)

D 1 mean, 2 makes, 3 surely, 4 in, 5 agree, 6 feelings/sentiments, 7/8 instance/example, 9 say, 10 if, 11 see, 12 concerned, 13 point, 14 nothing, 15 contrary, 16 relevant, 17/18 nonsense/rubbish

E 1st Gilbey, 2nd Feldheim, 3rd Kleindienst, 4th Masson, 5th Schmeichel, 6th Grandjean, 7th Mancini, 8th Miche

F This is a sample of a competition entry you might write:

Two weeks ago an English friend took me to watch my first cricket match. On the way to the ground he spent hours explaining the rules of the game, but when we arrived, I think I was more confused than ever.

The game began at eleven. Eleven men walked smartly on to the field, took up their positions and then waited until two of the opponents marched to the middle to meet them. These two men looked like something from a Mad Max movie, with helmets on their heads and padding all over their bodies.

For about six hours nothing much happened. Mad Max people came and went, there was a break of about 45 minutes and the teams changed around. My friend informed me that the first team had scored a total of 254 runs and now the other team had to score that number from the fixed number of balls bowled to them. With 60 more balls to go, the second team needed 70 more runs, and with 40 left, they needed 55. I started to jump up and down with everybody else.

The last five minutes were incredible . The last man with the bat had to score three runs from the last ball. He hit it high in the air and started running. However, a very tall young man from the other team ran about 100 metres in 10 seconds and caught the ball! — which meant that his team won the match, I think. Yes, it was exciting — in a way — in the end.

PROGRESS TEST 3 (Units 11–15)

A This is a sample of the letter you should aim to write:

Dear José,

Thanks a lot for your letter. It was great to hear from you after all this time. Sorry to hear you're unemployed at the moment. I'm sure you won't be for long. Talking of which, I spotted an advertisement in the window of a local travel agency the other day which might interest you.

It was advertising vacancies for three Adventure Holiday Guides to take people to places like the Sahara Desert, the Himalayas and the Amazon. You reminded me in your letter that you were a great traveller and I thought this might be the sort of thing you were looking for. They're looking for someone who speaks two languages apart from English — they mention Spanish, German and French — and someone who doesn't mind fighting the elements, solving problems for other people, and so on. Sounds just like you. They don't mention salary or working conditions, but I imagine they'd pay quite well.

Why don't you write to them? Oh, and send a CV. Their address is: The Adventure Holiday Company, Box 3000, London NW10.

Let me know if you do, and if so, whether they offer you a job. I don't see how they could say 'no' with your experience!

Give my regards to Joanna.

All best wishes, [207 words]

B a 6, **b** 3, **c** 8, **d** 2, **e** 7, **f** 4 (1 and 5 do not fit)

C1 1 A, C, D, 2 B, C, E, F, H, 3 B, C, E, 4 A, D, 5 B, C, D, 6 A, C, D. [B could only work if the first sentence were a question.] 7 A, C, F, 8 A, B.

C2 1A, 2A, 3C, 4B, 5A, 6D, 7D, 8C, 9B, 10C

C3 1 our company was being heralded

2 we were given a European Industries Award

3 Sno-trek is being left behind by its competitors.

4 We have been overtaken by certain companies

5 we are being beaten by other companies

6 what can be done about it?

7 our promotional activities (should) be re-evaluated

8 our designers (should) be given more scope

9 our representatives in the market are not being given

10 they had always been provided

Progress Test 3: Scoring Scheme

To mark and score the Progress Test, we suggest this simple
scoring scheme: Maximum

A	See Progress Test 1	
	Total possible maximum for **A**	40
B	6 items x 2 points each	12
C 1	24 items correct x 1 point each (1 for each correct option chosen)	24
2	10 items x 1 points each	10
3	10 items x 2 points each	20
	Total possible maximum for **C**	54

Unit 16   Body matters

A Possible sentences:

1 There is every likelihood that he will take some time to recover from the operation.

2 If you do a lot of sport the chances are that you will have the occasional injury.

3 She's very likely to recover in time for the concert.

4 The odds are that no two doctors will treat this rare condition in the same way.

5 There is every likelihood that people will eventually suffer from the same illnesses as their parents.

6 There's a (strong) chance that she'll pick up some strange infection there.

B 1 Babies born very prematurely...

2 ... people with/suffering from arthritis in their feet.

3 ... restaurants specialising in vegetarian food.

4 Anyone noticing an unusual lump in their body ...

5 People not used to the sun ...

6 People likely to be exposed to radioactivity at work ...

C 1 ... ought <u>to</u> put ...

2 ... you'd better take (N.B. no 'to')

3 ... the first thing to do is (<u>to</u>) <u>put</u> him ...

4 ... you must keep ... (N.B. no 'to')

5 ... advise that anyone with a serious problem go / should go ...

or ... advise anyone with a serious problem to go ...

6 Don't forget to check ...

D 1 The article will be about a baby born to a pop star.

2 This article will discuss ways to combat depression.

3 This article will be about the death of an elderly person.

4 This article will show how the sport of fencing helps people to become slimmer

5 This article will be about an argument (or perhaps legal proceedings?) over the hygiene/cleanliness at a pizza parlour/restaurant.

6 This article will be about a sports person whose shoulder was dislocated. The incident stopped the game.

7 This article will be about a cure for insomnia.

8 This article will discuss what kind of buildings suffer from what is known as sick building syndrome, which refers to having characteristics that tend to make people who live or work in such buildings ill.

E 1 g, 2 a, 3 f, 4 b, 5 e, 6 c.

F 1 imbalance, 2 allergic, 3 shooting, 4 tension, 5 dislocate, 6 symptoms, 7 prescribe, 8 cells, 9 stressful, 10 spine, 11 rundown, 12 lethargic, 13 infection, 14 physical, 15 surfeit, 16 hassles, 17 stress, 18 diet.

The doctor might take your <u>blood pressure</u> and your <u>pulse</u>.

G Open-ended.

Unit 17   Love makes the world go round

A 1 c, g, k, 2 j, 3 a, e, 4 k, 5 a, i, 6 b, j, 7 h, 8 l, 9 a, e, 10 c, g, k, 11 b, f, 12 h, 13 g, k, 14 i, 15 c, g, k, 16 c, g, 17 b, 18 b, f, j.

B 1 I need a thing for grating cheese. / ... (that) I can (use to) grate cheese with. / ... to grate cheese with.

2 I'm looking for something for keeping cutlery in. / ... (that) I can (use to) keep cutlery in. (The latter would probably sound more natural.) / ... to keep cutlery in.

3 I want a thingumajig for getting the core out of an apple. / ... (that) I can (use to) get the core out of an apple. / ... to get the core out of an apple with.

4 I need a tool for undoing nuts. / ... (that) I can (use to) undo nuts with. / ... to undo nuts with.

C Group 1 nouns are formed with a particle (*back-, down-, in-,* etc.) + verb, and the stress is on the particle.
Group 2 nouns are formed with a verb + particle, and the stress is on the verb.
1 outcome, 2 uprising, 3 letdown, 4 slip-up, 5 outlook, 6 onset, 7 hold-up, 8 offspring

D 1 I'll give everyone a handout.
2 I'll send you a printout.
3 There has been a (mass) breakout from the high-security prison.
4 There were very few onlookers.
5 There was a hold-up at the bank.
6 There has been an outbreak of cholera in the area.
7 There's been another slip-up.
8 I wanted a lie-in on Sunday.

E 1 The result of the talks is still uncertain.
2 The police are promising/have promised tough action on crime.
3 The President has denied hiding anything/information.
4 More people in the coal industry are going to be made redundant.
5 Economists (?)/experts(?)/politicians(?)/have promised that the economy will improve soon.
6 All (or most of) the workers in the docks have walked out.

F 2 The writer says that television advertisers use the interest of viewers in romance to sell products. TV commercials exploit the interest in love and romance by creating *either* an adventure story in which the hero risks all to bring the heroine the advertised product *or* a serial based on a boy/girl relationship. The writer is sceptical about how much such ads actually sell, but admires the standard of the product.

3 This is a sample of the kind of letter you should aim to write:

Dear Sir,

I was interested in the article 'Love sells coffee and chocolates — or does it?' which you published in last week's issue of your magazine.

In my opinion the writer is wrong to doubt the selling power of such advertisements as he describes. Companies spend enormous sums of money on the production of these commercials; their hard-headed managers would not do so if they did not have evidence to prove that sales would increase as a result of their expenditure.

What interests me is the way that people's love of — or at least interest in — animals is also used by British advertisers as a means of attracting custom. A particularly successful series of adverts was one made for electricity. These adverts all featured various domestic animals discussing the pleasures of having, say, central heating or a dishwasher. Their conversations were the very realistic, rather trivial small talk to be heard anywhere in the British Isles, but coming from the mouths of animals they were both amusing and effective.

A loveable shaggy dog always features in the popular Dulux paint adverts too. One of the most striking of these was the one where the dog causes his master to step in his can of paint just as he has completed painting his room. Again humour, then, combines neatly with an affectionate use of animals.

I wonder whether any other country uses love for animals as well as for people to sell its products?
Yours faithfully,   [244 words]

Unit 18   There's no accounting for taste

A 1 I can't stand people talking about me behind my back.
2 I'd prefer to go to the exhibition rather than the concert.
3 I'd rather you didn't say anything.
4 I wish you hadn't (gone and) told him.
5 I hate to say this, but I'm afraid you're not up to it.
6 What worries me about getting old is the effect it has on your mind. *or* The effect it has on your mind is what worries me about getting old.
7 It was so horrible I couldn't bear to watch/look.
8 The only thing I don't like about the CAE is the time limits. *or* The time limits are the only thing I don't like about the CAE.

B 1 for/in, 2 towards/to, 3 for, 4 in, 5 of, 6 after, 7 of, 8 with, 9 with, 10 in, 11 at, 12 on, 13 about, 14 of, 15 in, 16 in, 17 to, 18 of, 19 as, 20 in, 21 without

C 1 essential, 2 take, 3 possessions/belongings, 4 few, 5 however, 6 value/worth, 7 Consequently, 8 majority, 9 inadequate/insufficient, 10 advisable/sensible, 11 excess, 12 bearing, 13 replacing/replacement, 14 counts/matters, 15 advised, 16 idea, 17 advice, 18 case, 19 such, 20 present, 21 make, 22 contact/consult, 23 delay, 24 regret

D   Complimentary   Uncomplimentary

	Complimentary		Uncomplimentary
1	elegant	1	appalling
2	appealing	2	dreadful
3	superb	3	grotesque
4	splendid	4	horrendous
5	pleasant	5	awful
6	great	6	hideous

E This is a sample of the kind of letter you should aim to write:

Dear Sir or Madam,

I am writing to express my disappointment and dissatisfaction with the goods I ordered from you on 18th November.

Not one of the items I received this morning is in a satisfactory condition. Of the set of six dinner plates, two were cracked and one was chipped, making the set totally unusable. The handle of one of the pots broke off as soon as I touched it, and my 'beautifully crafted' pen doesn't write. My self-assembly CD and video stacking unit cannot be assembled because of missing or unsuitable accessories, the kitchen scales are wholly unreliable, and the trainers you sent are two sizes too small.

As all these items were supposed to be Christmas presents and since I clearly cannot trust you to send proper replacements in the next eight days, I should like to ask for a full refund of £153.41. Perhaps you could also arrange for the goods you sent to be collected.

I look forward to hearing from you.

Yours faithfully,   [164 words]

Unit 19   I didn't read what it said!

A 1 ✓, 2 would I do, 3 ✓, 4 the vegetables should be, 5 ✓, 6 ✓, 7 they had arrived, 8 I can never understand

B 1 when, 2 and, 3 that, 4 than, 5 as/since/because, 6 and/when, 7 that, 8 so, 9 that, 10 however/though, 11 when, 12 because/after

C 1 scratch, 2 Dip, 3 scald, 4 stirring, 5 simmer, 6 wiped, 7 whisk, 8 to scrub, 9 grazing, 10 rubbed

D 1 Kitchen equipment — tin opener, saucepan, kettle, mixer, skewer

2 Tools — saw, plane, chisel, spanner, drill

3 Car — fuel tank, engine, radiator, fanbelt, exhaust (pipe)

4 Containers — packet, box, tin, can, bag

5 Garden tools — fork, lawn mower, hedge-trimmer, trowel

6 Computers — mouse, disk drive, monitor, modem, keyboard

E a handlebars, b brake, c pedals, d saddle, e tyre, f mudguard, g chain, h bell, i spokes, j wheel, k pump, l crossbar, m light.

F 2 l, 3 k, 4 a, 5 h, 6 j, 7 g, 8 c, 9 e, 10 d, 11 b

G 1 ~~on~~, 2 ~~not~~, 3 ✓, 4 ~~most~~, 5 ~~into~~, 6 ~~can~~, 7 ✓, 8 ~~of~~

H Here are samples of what you might aim to write:

How to do a somersault

Kneel on the ground with the balls of your feet and the palms of your hands pressed onto the ground.
Curl your head underneath your body so that the top and back of your head touch the ground.
Push with your arms and feet so that your legs move round in a circle over your head and you turn over as if you were a ball rolling over. You end up sitting on the ground.

How to use a tape-recorder

Press the button to open the cassette compartment of the recorder.
Put in a cassette and close the compartment.
Press the play button if you want to listen to a recording.
Press the record button if you want to make a new recording.
The rewind button allows you to go back to the beginning of the cassette.
The fast forward button allows you to move forward quickly to the end of the cassette.

How to ride a bike

Sit on the saddle of the bike with one foot on one pedal, the toes of the other foot on the ground and your hands on the handlebars.
Push with the foot on the pedal so that the wheels start turning.
Swing the second foot onto the other pedal and then push each foot in turn so that you are pedalling the bike and making it go forwards.
Steer the bike by moving the handlebars, turning them in the direction you want to go in.
When you want to go more slowly or to stop, press the brake handle gently towards the handlebars.

Unit 20   Into the future!

A These are samples of the 'stories' — in random order:

1   Well, I'm leaving my present company at the end of the week. This time on Friday I'll be clearing my desk and saying goodbye to colleagues. And this time next week I'll have started work in my new job and will no doubt be trying to get used to new faces, new systems and so on.

2   My elder sister is getting married on Saturday. Just think, forty-eight hours from now she'll be standing at the altar, worrying about getting the words right, trying to keep calm. And by this time on Sunday, they'll have set off on their honeymoon and will probably be waiting at the airport for their flight to the Bahamas.

3   I'm taking my final college exams next week. In fact, this time on Tuesday I'll be sitting in the examination hall, just getting ready to do the first paper. It's only four days though. By Friday lunchtime I'll have finished the last paper and we'll be heading for the nearest restaurant.

4   I'm going to Los Angeles for the first time the day after tomorrow. Just think, in 48 hours' time, I'll be sitting on the aeroplane looking down over the Atlantic. And by the time you wake up on Saturday, I'll have landed in California and will be on my way to the hotel.

B This is a sample of what you might aim to write:

<u>The Road to the Future</u>

A major revolution has already started in what we drive and how we drive it. Already computers have to some extent begun to take over the driver's work, assessing and recording the car's performance and giving visual or spoken warnings when things are going wrong. This is of particular use in, say, long-distance lorry driving where a check can be kept that the vehicle is obeying all transport regulations. Another high-tech development to help motorists is the way that garages can now be built underground, under people's lawns or drives. This serves not only to save space but also to prevent car thefts and to reduce corrosion.

   More technological developments are in the pipeline and should be with us soon. It is reported that our cars will soon be equipped with computers that will judge the correct distance we should be from the car in front and may even, if our car is rather close to the next one, adjust the car's position so that it is at a safer distance. More sophisticated alarm systems to warn of danger are also currently being developed. These include such things as sensors which detect when a driver is unfit to drive, when he or she is, say, too sleepy. These sensors would then automatically trigger something to help keep the driver awake; it might, for instance, dispense a perfume or switch the air conditioning on and off.

So much has already happened or is about to happen that it is easy to believe that even more remarkable things will one day be possible. Experts are predicting that some time in the not too distant future, computers will be used to programme our car journeys so that drivers need to do little or nothing; it will be as if cars, like aeroplanes today, can simply be put on to auto-pilot. Then perhaps engines will be able to correct themselves, requesting replacement spare parts as they become necessary.

   Finally, it may become possible for drivers to fill up their cars with petrol and pay for it without getting out of the car. This was, of course, the normal practice twenty years ago when a garage assistant provided this service for drivers. In the future, however, the fill-up and payment will be carried out by means of an automatic machine. These are just some of the technological developments which will benefit motorists. I wonder what others have not yet even been dreamt of?

C Possible answers:

1   We feel that it is ridiculous that we should be asked to consider a reduction in salary.

2   There is not a grain of truth in the suggestion that we are deliberately trying to cause trouble.

3   It is only natural that we should want/wish to achieve better working conditions.

4   Unless management is prepared to improve their offer we shall be obliged/forced to take industrial action.

5   You may try to explain it away by blaming world recession, but we shall not be deterred from our proposed course of action/dissuaded from taking action.

6   Your attempts to adopt a stricter approach to staff absence are doomed to failure/have no chance of being successful.

7   We do not feel it is right that we should be blamed/be made the scapegoats for the difficulties you are having with your suppliers.

8   Basically it all boils down to whether we trust each other or not.

9   You can't talk us out of our claim./…our claiming what's due to us.

10 You've got to face up to the fact that none of us will accept voluntary redundancy/give up our job voluntarily.

11 We're not going to put up with this state of affairs any longer.

D 1 l, 2 a, 3 e, 4 g, 5 k, 6 h, 7 d, 8 b, 9 m, 10 f.

PROGRESS TEST 4 (Units 16–20)

A This is a sample of the letter you should aim to write:

Dear Mrs Ginelli,

As you will no doubt have discovered by now, a few things went wrong while my friends and I were at the Villa Rosanne and we felt we should write and try to explain.

Your instructions were very clear. However, we had a small problem when we wanted to do some washing. We may have put too much washing into the drum, it's possible we did not select the correct programme, or we might have omitted to put the washing-powder into the correct compartment on the machine — whatever it was, when we closed the front of the machine and finally started it, water poured out all over the floor. We cleared it up as well as we could, and sincerely hope that it did not do too much damage.

Your instructions about watering the plants were excellent, too. The problem was, I'm afraid, that we each thought the others were watering them — so I don't think they were watered at all. If you would like us to buy new plants to replace the old ones, please let us know.

And one more apology. Your instructions stated quite clearly that the villa keys should be left with Mr Dean at the local store. I know the front and back doors were locked securely. I did it myself. Unfortunately, I found the keys in the bottom of my bag when I got home. I am enclosing them.

I can only apologise most sincerely once again for everything that went wrong and say that we shall be prepared to pay for any damage we caused.

I look forward to hearing from you.

Yours sincerely,   [269 words]

B 1 f, 2 a, d, g, 3 c, 4 b, 5 e, 6 c, d

C1 1A, 2D, 3B, 4D, 5A, 6C, 7D, 8C, 9C, 10D

C2 1 It's not very likely/It's highly unlikely that that will happen.

2 You'd be well advised not to mention it to her./You'd better not mention it to her.

3 Hadn't we better knock first before we go in?

4 We'll get nowhere if we spend so long on each point.

5 I'd prefer to save my money rather than spend it on rubbish like that.

6 No sooner had she finished one sweet than she ate/would eat another.

7 All four batteries should/must be removed from the radio and (should/must be) replaced with new ones.

8 I'd rather you didn't mention it again.

9 I wish I had been to China.

10 Apart from losing his job last week, he also lost a lot of money gambling.

C3 1 symptoms, 2 ingredients, 3 crushing, 4 specifically, 5 ✓, 6 ✓, 7 abominable, 8 fever, 9 pouring, 10 horrendous

C4 Possible version:

1 Pull the 'Open Cover' lever towards you. Lift the cover until the weight is on the support arm.

2 Take the wrapping off the roll of paper and place the roll into the shallow compartment.

3 Feed the end of the paper under the paper guide. The paper will come out under the front of the machine.

4 Close the cover firmly but gently until it clicks into position.

5 The fax machine will then feed the thermal paper through and cut off a short length automatically.

Progress Test 4: Scoring Scheme

To mark and score the Progress Test, we suggest this simple scoring scheme:

		Maximum
A	See Progress Test 1	
	Total possible maximum for **A**	40
B	9 answers x 2 points each	18
C 1	10 items x 1 point each	10
2	10 items x 2 points each	20
3	10 items x 1 point each	10
4	5 sentences x 2 points each	10
	Total possible maximum for **C**	50

SECTION C: ENGLISH IN USE

Time: 40 minutes

1 Choose the best word or phrase to fill the blanks — A, B, C or D.

1 The problem . . . . if we had kept an eye on things more carefully.
   A wouldn't arise   B hadn't arisen
   C wouldn't have arisen   D won't arise

2 Of course, by doing that we run the risk . . . . the contract.
   A to lose   B of losing   C lose   D losing

3 When you were younger, ... to have to walk to school?
   A did you use   B were you used   C had you
   D did you ever

4 She was always made . . . . after meals when she was younger.
   A wash up   B washing up   C to wash up
   D to have washed up

5 I can clearly recall my parents . . . . for me at the bus station that day.
   A while they waited   B the way they waited
   C wait   D waiting

6 . . . . time went by, she slowly got used to her new lifestyle.
   A Soon   B Before   C As   D While

7 . . . . then what I know now, I would not have invited them.
   A Were I known   B If I knew   C Had I known
   D Knowing them

8 She is . . . . the best singer I've heard for a long time.
   A by far   B a lot   C considerably   D rather

9 She has a lot . . . . her brother.
   A in common with   B identical to
   C similar to   D equal with

10 They . . . . for an hour when the bus finally arrived.
   A waited   B were waiting   C had been waiting
   D would have waited

2 Fill each of the numbered blanks in the following passage with **one** word.

'As far as I can see,' Inspector Tage said, 'it's an open and (1). . . . . case. The evidence is here in (2). . . . . and white in the old man's will.'

'Well, I don't know how his daughter put (3). . . . . with him all these years,' said the Sergeant. 'And I know he (4). . . . . out with his son years ago. The son told me himself he couldn't live (5). . . . . to his father's expectations of him. He took (6). . . . . his mother too much. But I still don't see —'

'I'll try to explain. First of all, the trouble with the son was (7). . . . . and buried years ago. Perhaps we'll never know the ins and (8). . . . . of it, but it's not important. The family might have fought (9). . . . . and nail and might have broken (10). . . . . for a while, but they were a family, and even families that grow (11). . . . . get together again in times of crisis. It's all (12). . . . . and parcel of family life, that sort of thing, isn't it?'

'So what you're saying, Inspector, is: they all got together when the old man fell ill. If so, that turns *my* theory (13). . . . . down.'

'Well, your theory was a bit hit and (14). . . . . anyway. It wouldn't have (15). . . . . up to much scrutiny.'

3 Write the correct form of the pairs of words in brackets to complete the sentences.

1 She was (deep/offend) by his remarks.

. . . .

2 That boy has an (exception/talent).

. . . .

3 There was an (awkward/silent) as we entered.

. . . .

4 He might be (physical/handicap), but he's a great athlete.

. . . .

5 She was (infinite/pretty) than I had imagined.

. . . .

6 The fruit can't have gone bad. The jar was (hermetic/seal).

. . . .

7 By the time the sun went down, we realised we were (hopeless/lose).

. . . .

8 She has a (price/collect) of jewels.

. . . .

9 They've been (happy/marry) for 50 years.

. . . .

10 There has been (increase/press) on the sea eagle's habitat during the past century.

. . . .

4 You're writing the biography of a famous person (Ron, a pop group keyboard player) and have been lent some diaries from his early teens (the mid-1980s). This is an extract from one of them. Read it and do the exercise below.

SUNDAY, 5TH JUNE

I've broken out in spots again, and they'll make me go to school again tomorrow, I know they will! They always do, and it really gets me! It's bad enough blushing and stammering every time I speak to H. She has that effect on me. She's been encouraging me — with her eyes, and her body language. I'm heavily into body language — been reading a good book about it. Doesn't help me. Bob and his crowd (I hate them!) are always making fun of my attempts to get off with H. I'll show them one day.

I've been trying to learn to play the guitar for 6 months but have realised it's not for me, so I'm chucking it in. It's the keyboard next. I spent 2 hours yesterday in the music shop in town and have decided to save up for a Yamaha. They might take my guitar as a deposit — you never know.

I'm determined to buy one and by this time next year I will have joined a group!!

Now, on a separate piece of paper, complete the paragraph for the biography, keeping as close to the original as you can, and beginning like this:

One Sunday in early June of that year Ron had broken out in spots again and knew that his parents would make him go to school on the Monday morning. They always insisted on him going, and he resented it. . . .

All in a day's work

Grammar

A A number of people wrote why they went into their professions. Column A shows the first part of what they said; column C gives sentences from advertisements for different professions. Sort them out and, on a separate piece of paper, write each in full, joining the ideas with an appropriate word or phrase from box B. There are several possible answers in each case. Try to use as many of the phrases in box B as you can.

0 *e) I decided to do community work in order to help people in society.*

A	B	C
0 'I decided to do community work ...'	in case	a Help cure terrible diseases.
1 'I became a sailor ...'	with a view to	b Play in an orchestra! Don't teach!
2 'I became self-employed ...'	to	c Set up your own management advice bureau.
3 'I trained as an artist ...'	so as to	d Use your languages.
4 'I did a management course ...'	so as not to	e Help people in society.
5 'I became a bilingual secretary ...'	in order to	f Why not be a professional cartoonist?
6 'I originally went into acting ...'	in order not to	g See the world!
7 'I went into medical research ...'	so that	h How about becoming a film producer?
8 'I became a professional violinist ...'		i Don't take orders from others! Work for yourself.

B Below each of these sentences there are four options. Circle all the options that will fit in the sentence.

0 It . . . . work . . . soon.

   a will rain   **b** is going to rain   **c** rains   **d** will be raining

1 We . . . . in the swimming pool every Friday afternoon from now on.

   a train   **b** are training   **c** will be training   **d** are going to train

2 The coach . . . . at precisely 8 a.m. on Friday. Please don't be late.

   a is leaving   **b** leaves   **c** will leave   **d** is going to leave

3 If you ring him at about 7, I'm pretty sure he . . . . dinner.

   a has   **b** is having   **c** will have   **d** will be having

4 I'm sure she . . . . soon.

   a is promoted   **b** will be promoted   **c** is going to be promoted
   d is being promoted

Writing

C You work for a large travel company and have been asked to write some questions for a questionnaire to find out something about the office employees' ambitions, hopes and fears. Write these first few questions out in full from the notes.

0 hope — promoted — next 3 years?
   Do you hope to be promoted in the next three years? ....

1 ever been afraid — made redundant?

   ....

2 intend — stay with company — long time?

   ....

3 every fancy — manage one of our branches abroad?

   ....

4 dread — asked — be a courier?

   ....

5 any intention — leave company — next 2 years?

   ....

Write **four more questions** of your own to add to the questionnaire. Use the verbs *aim*, *loathe* and *expect*, and the adjective *anxious*.

Vocabulary

D Match the prefixes in box A with words in box B and write them on a separate piece of paper. Each of the prefixes in box A can go before at least two of the words in box B.

| **A** sub- self- anti- co- pro- part- super- high- low- |

| **B** committee educational owner flier human confident level American pitched calibre aqua employed freeze efficient time reform social director |

E Now choose words from the list you made in **D** to fill the blanks in these sentences.

0 He made a ..... *super-human* .... effort to save the boy, but failed.

1 She's the .... of a restaurant. She and some others own about 10% each.

2 It's such a .... whistle only dogs can hear it.

3 He's so .... he never even speaks to his next-door neighbour.

4 The directors formed a special .... to look into the matter.

5 The company only wants .... people for its sales force.

Reading

F Read this passage and do the exercises below.
IMPORTANT NOTE: There are five printing mistakes in it. Watch out for them as you read.

High-flying job-sharers

Liz Bray and Susan Burns are a manager — and if that sounds grammatically odd, let me quickly explain.

5 Liz and Susan are just two of thousands of women who now share a job as the ideal answer to that age-old problem of how to follow a
10 career and look after a home and bring up children.

They first met when they each answered an advertisement for the same
15 position — Personnel Manager for an investment group. They both had the same qualifications and the same interests, were roughly
20 the same age, and were thrilled when they were both offered the job. But before they took on the job share, they both agreed to a
25 probationary period.

They wouldn't divulge what they earn between them, but they are both high-fliers, and the position is an
30 extremely responsible one, so the salary must be substantial. They each take 50% of the total. They both work three-fifths of the time,
35 and neither wants to oust the other. After all, Liz's job depends on Susan's work, and vice versa, so neither is at all scarred that the other
40 might want to take over the whole job.

As to the mechanics of job-sharing, Liz and Susan both work on Mondays —
45 'It's vital to have some overlap time,' said Liz emphatically — then Liz works on Tuesdays and Thursdays, and Susan works
50 Wednesdays and Fridays. When I met them, it was a Monday morning and they were siting at a large desk discussing recent applica-
55 tions for a post in the Marketing Department.

They admit they both used to have petty quarrels with colleagues in previous
60 positions. Not in this one. They might have disagreements, but when I was interviewing them, there were no
65 waging fingers!

'I thought I might be bared from a job like this,' said Liz, 'simply because I couldn't devote my whole
70 time to it. I'd applied for numerous positions of this calibre, but they'd all turned me down once they knew I had three young children.
75 This has come as a marvellous opportunity.'

And when asked about 'the executive image', Susan told me: 'We don't wear the
80 typical executive's stripped suit, although I do occasionally come in a smart navy-blue costume.'

1 What were the five printing mistakes? How should the words have been spelt?

2 Suggest alternative ways of expressing these words and phrases from the passage:
a) thrilled (1.21)   b) probationary (1.25)   c) divulge (1.26)
d) substantial (1.32)   e) oust (1.35)   f) the mechanics of (1.42)
g) emphatically (1.47)   h) petty (1.58)   i) numerous (1.71)

3 Are these statements about Liz and Susan True or False? — or aren't we told?

	True	False	Not told
a) They had both been Personnel Managers before.	. . . . .	. . . . .	. . . . .
b) They earn a large salary between them.	. . . . .	. . . . .	. . . . .
c) They split the job 60%–40%.	. . . . .	. . . . .	. . . . .
d) Their jobs overlap on a Monday.	. . . . .	. . . . .	. . . . .
e) It is possible they disagree occasionally.	. . . . .	. . . . .	. . . . .

12 *The persuaders*

Grammar

A In these lines from various advertisements, some of the gaps need *the*, *that* or *who*, some of them don't. Fill in the gaps if a word is *really needed*; otherwise put in a dash.

Are you looking for ...	
	0 a toy . . . — . . you can give to . . — . . toddlers and . . *the* . . not-so-young?
	1 **a car . . . . has . . . . gadgets . . . . you've never even dreamed of and . . . . power you've always wanted?**
	2 a powder . . . . you can use at all . . . . temperatures for . . . . weekly wash?
	3 a travel agent . . . . can be relied on to tell you . . . . truth, not . . . . lies?
	4 a TV channel . . . . keeps you up to date with . . . . information about . . . . politics, ... current affairs and . . . . latest in . . . . fashion?

B Write 'C' against the nouns below which are countable, 'U' against those which are always (or nearly always) uncountable, and 'C/U' against those which can easily be both. Use a dictionary if you want to.

0 **a** accommodation . *U* . . **b** information . *U* . . **c** action *C/U*
  d starvation . *U* . .

1 **a** furniture . . . . . **b** picture . . . . . **c** feature . . . . .
  d brochure . . . . . **e** leisure . . . . . **f** nature . . . . .
  g culture . . . . . **h** literature . . . . .

2 **a** spaghetti . . . . . **b** confetti . . . . . **c** broccoli . . . . .
  d macaroni . . . . . **e** salami . . . . . **f** chilli . . . . . **g** kiwi . . . . .
  h taxi . . . . .

3 **a** mathematics . . . . . **b** physics . . . . . **c** genetics . . . . .
  d politics . . . . . **e** news . . . . . **f** gymnastics . . . . .

4 **a** progress . . . . . **b** heiress . . . . . **c** distress . . . . .
  d watercress . . . . .

C   **A** too little   **B** too few   **C** too much   **D** too many
Which of these phrases would you use with the nouns below to describe conditions in some countries? Write the appropriate letter A, B, C or D next to each word.

0 . . *C* . . . poverty
1 . . . . . . schools
2 . . . . . . education
3 . . . . . . unscrupulous politicians
4 . . . . . . soldiers
5 . . . . . . fighting
6 . . . . . . hospitals
7 . . . . . . technical know-how
8 . . . . . . specialists
9 . . . . . . babies being born
10 . . . . . . hope

Style and register

D Below is a list of phrases which are (or might be) euphemisms — polite forms. Write beside each one a straightforward version of the phrase.

0 (people who are) not very well off ... *poor* ......
1 (a person) of below average height ....
2 (a person who is) somewhat overweight ....
3 (bread that is) less than fresh ....
4 (a student) of questionable ability ....
5 (a room that looks) lived-in ....
6 (a player who is) past his best ....
7 (a professor who is) slightly eccentric ....
8 (a film) of dubious merit ....
9 (a politician who is) economical with the truth ....
10 unsightly refuse disposal units ....

E Which of these ten much stronger (probably ruder) expressions can you match with 1–10 above? Write the number beside each phrase below.

a hopeless ... *4* ...
b as big round as he is tall ......
c a mess ......
d an eyesore ......
e a has-been ......
f a midget ......
g as hard as rock ......
h rubbish ......
i as mad as a hatter ......
j a liar ......

Vocabulary

F Use one of these verbs in an appropriate form to complete the sentences below.

> record show ✓ handle wash sell read corner
> photograph crease work stain ✓ hold

0 Light-coloured carpets ... *stain* ...... very easily; every mark *shows* ....

1 This material .... very easily and it doesn't .... very well.

2 Your composition .... very well but the ending doesn't ....

3 These new flats aren't .... very well and house prices in general aren't .... up.

4 Her voice .... very well and she .... very well, too.

5 The car .... beautifully and .... so smoothly.

Reading

..... A **Recommended by top breeders everywhere!**

..... B Goes on easily, straight from the fridge!

..... C *Chew what you choose from now on!*

..... D **Half a billion people can't be wrong every day, can they?**

..... E *Brand-new formula for extra body and bounce!*

..... F Today's technology in tomorrow's body!

G Read this passage and then match the products which the writer mentions (0–9) with the advertising slogans of these products (A–J). Write the numbers beside the letters.

Is there something wrong with me? My least favourite drink (0) is the one that the ad implies is drunk by the most daredevil, macho men in the land. I hate the instant coffee (1) advertised by one of Britain's most popular screen couples. When I eat anything with a particular denture fixative (2) in place, I find I spend more time negotiating dentures than food, despite the fact that I am promised an enjoyable, embarrassment-free meal by the suppliers. After washing it with a shampoo/ conditioner combination (3), my hair looks like that of a straw doll. The car (4) I drive — when it starts — and am desperately keen to get rid of is, I am assured, unbeatable value. I am usually so disfigured in the morning after five minutes in the bathroom with my revolutionary twin-blade razor (5) that what goes on my toast (6) — 'You'll notice the difference' — is a matter of complete indifference to me. Even our cat refuses to eat, except in emergency, the food (7) that would appear to be by far the most popular ever tinned. And yet I regularly find myself humming along to the jingle for the most advertised canned drink on earth (8), which apparently unites the world as no other drink can and which I find undrinkable. And I go on applying the 'guaranteed-to-act-fast' gel (9) on my winter cold sores, even though it patently increases their size and unsightliness. Is there anyone we can trust? Can we even trust ourselves?

.....0. H I bet he drinks bottles of Brown's Best!

.... I **River Deep Advantage — just add hot water and stir!**

..... G *Heals, soothes and gives instant relief!*

.... J **Gets closer than ever; now 5 o'clock shadow's a thing of the past!**

Writing

H You have just read that several 'environmentally-friendly' cosmetic products advertised regularly on television are in fact tested on live animals. Write a letter of complaint to the Managing Director (of the cosmetics company), claiming that what the company is doing is unethical and misleading to the public.

13 *Travel broadens the mind*

Grammar

A Which prepositions fit into the gaps in this text?

Driving in Hong Kong is a bit (0) ....*of*.......... a nightmare nowadays. I'm really glad that I live a stone's throw (1) .... my work. I should hate to have to spend hours every morning battling (2) .... traffic jams only to end up having to drive (3) .... and (4) .... for ages trying to find a parking space to squeeze myself (5) .... And you certainly can't take the risk (6) .... parking (7) .... the side of the road as you are quite likely to get a heavy fine if you do. More and more people are taking (8) .... their bicycles. There are rather too many hills in Hong Kong (9) .... my liking, however. It's all right going (10) .... but pedalling (11) .... them is too much (12) .... me first thing (13) .... the morning or last thing (14) .... night. And (15) .... so much traffic it's particularly hard (16) .... a bike when you are trying to get (17) .... or (18) .... a main road. It can't be good (19) .... your health breathing (20) .... all those petrol fumes either, although (21) .... least cyclists are helping the environment (22) .... not using cars.

Style and register

B The writer of this draft has tried to strike a formal tone. However, he has often not managed to find the right word or phrase to suit the style. Rewrite it on a separate piece of paper, choosing any appropriate words or phrases from the box below to replace the parts underlined. Make any other changes you think are necessary. Not all the options are required.

The great problem with (0) the arrival of the whole business of travel and catering for tourists is that, as has been proved on so many occasions, (1) the way the local residents have always lived is often immediately under threat. Many experts nowadays of course question (2) whether we really *need* tourism, and yet it is hardly a question when the search for ever more (3) places that are very attractive to visit continues. (4) The way things have been going in the past few years in the 'exotic adventure holiday' industry would seem to show that (5) people like such holidays more and more. It is those distant holiday destinations with (6) an economic system based mainly on the country and farming, however, that have suffered most from the intrusive interest of foreign visitors.

exotic locations / prove increasingly popular / traditional lifestyle / the advent of tourism ✓ / the desirability / small-scale developments / a predominantly rural-based economy / largely unexplored areas / recent developments / the infrastructure needed to accommodate visitors

Begin like this:
The great problem with (0) **the advent of tourism** is that ...

Vocabulary

C Which of the words and expressions below have positive and which have negative connotations? Mark them 'P' for positive or 'N' for negative.

destruction	*N*
hospitality	. . . . .
trim (adjective)	. . . . .
shoddy	. . . . .
picturesque	. . . . .
a drag	. . . . .
to relish	. . . . .
to shove	. . . . .
sparkling	. . . . .
brawling	. . . . .
to make a quick buck	. . . . .
lout	. . . . .
erosion	. . . . .
bland	. . . . .

D Now choose words or expressions from **C** to complete these sentences. Change the form of the words if necessary — e.g. put a verb into the appropriate tense.

0 The hotel was very . . . . . *shoddily* . . . . built.

1 We were showered with . . . . in Greece.

2 I'm just longing to plunge into those . . . . waters.

3 It's a . . . . having to spend most days going round museums with dad.

4 I don't . . . . the thought of having to walk to the village every day for milk.

5 If he cut his hair he wouldn't look such a . . . .

6 He'd sell his granny to . . . .

7 Please stop . . . . Ask and I'll move.

8 Because English food uses relatively few spices it can taste quite . . . .

9 The village is very . . . . situated in a little cove.

10 Although she's had six children, her figure is still very . . . .

E In these sentences one word is not quite right for the context. Underline it and then write a word which fits the context better.

0 We had a very enjoyable <u>travel</u> to France at the weekend. . . . . *trip* . . . .

1 The fly from London to New York only takes five hours. . . . .

2 Travel is said to widen your mind. . . . .

3 The doctor took me into his office to examine me. . . . .

4 Tourists have caused a lot of injury to the area. . . . .

5 The Minister sounded a word of warning in his speech last night. . . . .

6 My mother says that rich food doesn't fit with her. . . . .

7 My aunt was a hit-and-run sacrifice in an accident. . . . .

8 I can't remember his name — my brain's gone blank. . . . .

Reading

F A friend has gone on holiday and sent you this letter. Unfortunately, the numbered words are illegible. It is, however, possible to work out what those words probably are from their context. They are all words which collocate very strongly with the words beside them.

I'm having a fantastic time here. The hotel is literally a (0) *stone's* throw from the beach, and we are within easy walking (1) .... of a lovely little restaurant. The hotel is within easy (2) .... of a small town, too, although I don't much care for it. As is often the case, the needs of foreign visitors are clearly at (3) .... with the needs of the local people. Huge hotel blocks, cinemas, and souvenir shops have been built and it's all turned into a bit of a concrete (4) .... The locals say it used to be a peaceful and rather picturesque old town and that it's changed beyond all (5) .... Mind you, tourism has certainly had an enormous (6) .... on the country's economy. People certainly have more money now than they had in the past.

Writing

G This picture story shows the route of Jim and Jan's cycling holiday last year. The pictures show what happened at various points during their trip. Write about 250 words describing where they went and what happened to them. Refer to the pictures fully but use your imagination to fill in as many details as you wish. Begin like this: *'Last summer Jim and Jan went on a week's cycling holiday ...'*

16. A chapter of accidents

Grammar

A There was a terrible fire in the Hofburg Palace in Vienna in late November, 1992. Read what people told reporters at the time, then write what the reporters put in their articles. Begin with the words given in each case.

0 'The fire has destroyed the ballrooms.'

The ballrooms **have been destroyed**.

1 'Policemen saved many books from the national library.'

Many books . . . .

2 'I doubt if they'll ever rebuild it.'

'I doubt if it . . . .'

3 'They use the conference rooms for disarmament negotiations.'

The conference rooms . . . .

4 'They're slowly bringing the fire under control.'

The fire . . . .

5 'The fire didn't hurt anyone.'

No one . . . .

6 'They had led the Lippizaner horses out before the fire could reach them.'

The Lippizaner horses . . . .

B Supply an appropriate continuous form of the verbs in brackets — positive, negative or question. You might need *is/are (not) doing, was/were (not) doing, has/have (not) been doing, might (not) have been doing*, etc.

It happened when my friends and I (0) **were driving** (drive) home from a party one night last month. They (1). . . . . (all/drink), but I hadn't, so I can only think I (2). . . . . (must/dream). The first warning I had was when I heard Gino shout: 'What (3). . . . . (you/do)?!' I looked up and saw that a massive lorry (4). . . . . (come) straight at us! My first thought was 'I (5). (can't/drive) on the wrong side of the road. Other vehicles have passed us OK.' But I know now that I (6). . . . . (ought/watch) the road a lot more carefully, because in that split second I realised that we (7). (cross) the long narrow bridge that we had come over earlier in the evening. It was a single carriageway! My friends and I are lucky to be alive — in fact, we (8). . . . . (should all/play) harps in heaven! But somehow, and I still can't believe it, both the lorry driver and I managed to brake before we smashed into each other. Yes, I'm alive — but I (9). . . . . (not drive) again for a very long time! — But I (10). (not think) of giving up my driving licence just yet, either.

Vocabulary

C Match the 'collective' words in box A with words in box B (to form expressions like 'a block of flats'). Write them on a separate piece of paper. Use a dictionary if you want or need to.

> **A** chapter crowd pile flock herd pack team
> catalogue bunch chain fleet

> **B** disasters shops grapes cattle oil tankers accidents
> people wolves experts papers sheep

D Now fill the blanks in these sentences with appropriate phrases from your list.

0 Everything's gone wrong! The whole thing has been .. *a* ....
catalogue of disasters .... from beginning to end!

1 He owns .... and ....
.... ! It's not surprising he's a millionaire!

2 Those men are not just 'a crowd of people.' They know exactly what they're doing. They're ....

3 'Sorry we're late. First of all there was ....
on the road. Then only a mile away we got stuck behind ....
....

4 She eventually found her passport under ....
.... on the desk.

Writing

E You have been asked to write a short article for an English language magazine about recent terrible storms and flooding in a part of your country. Yesterday evening you rang a friend of yours who is living in the flooded area. The notes below are what you took down while talking to your friend on the telephone. Write the article on a separate piece of paper. Give it a suitable heading and begin:
'Yesterday afternoon the east coast of ...'

> *East coast hit by gales and high tides. Thousands of acres flooded – hundreds of people evacuated – higher ground. Rescue centres opened – people taken there. Hotels and holiday homes also flooded. Many cars also swept away. Two main roads into area – closed by police: reason – two bridges washed away. Visitors/ Holiday makers advised not to travel to area.*
>
> *Many injured – fortunately only one person drowned.*
>
> *Snow – blizzards forecast for tomorrow; all precautions being taken.*

Reading

F A week before the Hofburg Palace fire in November, 1992, fire swept through Windsor Castle. This is a brief account of what happened. There is a sentence or part of a sentence missing from each paragraph. The missing parts are all at the bottom of the page. Read the text and indicate which of the (part-)sentences (**a–h**) go where. Two of the options are not needed.

THE WINDSOR CASTLE FIRE

It was at 11.37 on the morning of 20 November, 1992, that the alarm was raised. A whisper of white smoke had been seen and the fire brigade was sent for. Fire engines arrived eleven minutes later, (1). . . . . , and castle staff and volunteers were already making human chains to bring out many of the priceless treasures.

The fire started in the Private Chapel in a corner of the castle, where the walls and curtains were quickly set alight. One of the first people to see it described it as an 'inferno'. Within minutes the fire had spread to the adjoining St George's Hall where the Queen used to hold state banquets (2). . . . .

No one is really sure how the fire started. (3). . . . That work included rewiring, and it is thought that the fire might have been caused by an electrical fault.

Whatever the cause, the fire did millions of pounds' worth of damage, (4). . . . These included paintings by Van Dyck and drawings by Leonardo and Holbein, all in the Queen's own priceless private art collection.

Because the fire spread so rapidly through a section of the castle, (5). . . . finally to bring it under control. They were still damping down the day after the fire started.

As a footnote, it has since been estimated (6). . . . something in the region of £40 million. Part of the bill will be met by the State, part will be paid by the Queen herself.

a workmen had been carrying out restoration work for the previous three years

b it took some 200 firefighters and 35 fire appliances

c and which was one of the last parts of the building to be renovated

d for firefighters from the neighbouring town of Windsor

e because the castle's fire-warning system was not effective enough

f although many great works of art were saved

g that the cost of restoration will be

h by which time flames could be seen from outside the famous castle

15 All work and no play ...

Grammar

A On a separate piece of paper, rewrite the sentences, using each of the given prompts in turn. For example:

0 You won't win unless you train hard.
   a) way b) question c) chance
   a) *The only way you'll win is if you train hard.*
   b) *Winning's out of the question unless you train hard.*
   or *There's no question of you(r) winning unless you train hard.*
   c) *You have no chance of winning unless you train hard.*

1 They nearly won.
   a) managed b) succeeded c) failed d) very close

2 It's a waste of time asking him.
   a) use b) point c) worth d) pointless

3 I had no difficulty (in) answering the questions.
   a) difficult b) trouble c) easy d) easily e) ease

B Put the verbs in brackets into a suitable form. (Sometimes more than one is possible.)

0 I remember, it was the first time I ... *had ridden/rode* ....
   (ride) on a double-decker bus.

1 This may be the last time we .... (ever meet).

2 That's the last time I .... (buy) anything from that shop.

3 This is only the second time I .... (ever eat) snails.

4 The first time I .... (speak) to him, I thought he was Irish.

5 The next time you .... (come), all this will have been forgotten.

6 It must have been the last time anyone ....
   (see) him alive.

7 This is the last time I .... (remind) you.

8 This is the first time I .... (ever be) in a helicopter.

9 This will be the first time I .... (ever try) to make ice-cream.

10 It was the only time he .... (ever go) climbing alone, and he had a bad fall.

Vocabulary

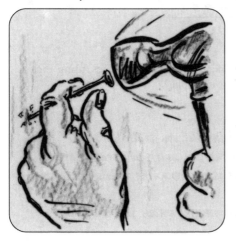

C Match each verb on the left with a suitable noun or phrase on the right. Then write short sentences on a separate piece of paper to illustrate the way some of the words can be used together.

0 .. **K** .. to hammer (in)	A	a meeting
1 ..... to foot	B	the issue
2 ..... to pocket	C	a book
3 ..... to cup	D	the bill
4 ..... to milk	E	a horse
5 ..... to saw	F	the ball
6 ..... to face	G	facts
7 ..... to boot	H	your hands
8 ..... to thumb (through)	I	a cow
9 ..... to shoe	J	the garden
10 ..... to chair	K	a nail ✓
11 ..... to water	L	the blame
12 ..... to shoulder	M	a film
13 ..... to paper	N	the wood
14 ..... to screen	O	your winnings
15 ..... to cloud	P	the bedroom

0 *I hammered the nail into the wall as hard as I could.*

Style and register

D In this informal argument, one word is missing from each utterance. Fill in the missing words.

A: (0) ..... **To** ..... my mind,
(0) ..... **In** ..... my view, } flying kites is a waste of time.

B: What do you (1) .... by that?
What (2) .... you say that?

A: Well, (3) ....
(4) .... my opinion, } there are better ways of spending your free time.

C: I couldn't (5) .... more.
My (6) .... exactly.

B: Like what, for { (7) .... ?
(8) .... ?

A: Well, (9) I'd ....
(10) .... you ask me, } almost anything is preferable to that.

C: As I (11) .... it,
As far as I'm (12) .... , } it's kids' stuff!

B: That's beside the (13) ....
That has (14) .... to do with it.

A: On the (15) .... ! I feel it's very (16) ....

D: Well, *I* think you're all talking { (17) .... !
(18) .... !

Reading

E Read this article and write down the surnames of the eight competitors in the order in which they came — from first to last.

FINAL POSITIONS

1st . . . .

2nd . . . .

3rd . . . .

4th . . . .

5th . . . .

6th . . . .

7th . . . .

8th . . . .

How the mighty are falling

The second day of the Hochdorf downhill Grand Prix left a number of top European skiers with a considerable amount of egg, not to mention snow, on their faces, none more than last year's winner Jean-Claude Miche, who for the second race running failed to complete the course.

Of the early starters, in poor skiing conditions, the Austrian Klaus Feldheim posted an exceptionally fast time, which for most of the day looked unlikely to be beaten. It was only when the penultimate competitor and hot favourite, Brad Gilbey of the United States, thundered down in 1 minute 52.01 seconds that Feldheim was edged from the top of the leader board.

Of the other fancied competitors, only Hans Schmeichel (Switzerland) made any kind of showing, but it is doubtful whether coming three places behind arch-rival Feldheim was a source of any satisfaction. An out-of-sorts Michel Grandjean (France) was well below his best, turning in a time of 1m. 54.78 secs., which might have qualified as the shock of the day had not Mario Mancini (Italy) later had a disastrous run which included at least three near-falls and left him over 5 seconds outside the next slowest finisher's time.

The newcomer to the Canadian team, Paul Masson, impressed again and was unlucky to be pipped for third place by a prodigious effort on the part of the German, Dieter Kleindienst, late in the day.

Writing

F You see this writing competition in a sports magazine.

Monthly Competition

Be a sports journalist for a day.

Write a report of about 250 words of an exciting sporting event you have attended or watched on television recently. Entries welcomed from writers whose mother tongue is not English.

Write your entry for the competition.

Progress Test 3 (Units 11–15)

SECTION A: WRITING

Time: 45 minutes

Scared of heights?

Hate the cold or searing heat?

Can't deal with other people's problems?

Can only speak English?

— **If so, this job is NOT for you!**

On the other hand,

- if you have a sense of adventure,
- if you have some experience of visiting remote parts of the world,
- if you love mountains,
- if you don't mind fighting the elements,
- if you are good at solving problems for others,
- **and** you can speak one or two other languages (French? German? Spanish?) as well as English —

then **WE NEED YOU!**

We are looking for three Adventure Holiday Guides to join our team of experienced couriers to accompany small parties visiting places as far apart as the Himalayas, the Sahara and the Amazon. Write, enclosing detailed CV, to:

THE *ADVENTURE HOLIDAY* COMPANY, Box 3000, London NW10

An acquaintance of yours has written to ask if you can help find him or her a job. Part of the letter is reproduced below. You have just spotted the advertisement (on the left) in the window of a travel agency. Referring to the letter extract and the advertisement, write a letter (about 200 words) to the writer telling him/her about the job and recommending that he/she apply. (Remember, you can't just send a photocopy of the ad. You must briefly describe the job.) **Write your answer on a separate piece of paper.**

> We haven't been in touch for a while, so you might be surprised to learn that I've just spent 18 months as the *Personnel Manager* in a small engineering company. I enjoyed it and did quite well, but the company went bust, so I'm unemployed.
>
> What I'm desperately looking for now is a job which is more than <u>just a job</u> — if you know what I mean!
>
> You know I'm still quite young, but you also know I'm already a veteran traveller. I've done all sorts — climbed mountains in the Andes, trekked across one of the hottest parts of Australia, been on two expeditions up the Amazon, visited just about every country in the Far East ... <u>And</u> I've learned to speak Spanish and German pretty fluently.
>
> So — if you hear of anything that might suit me, please let me know.

SECTION B: READING

Suggested time: 15 minutes

Read this text carefully. Six of the sentences 1–8 below summarise the six different paragraphs in the text. Match them with the paragraphs **a–f.** Remember, two of the suggested sentence summaries do not fit.

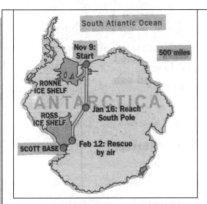

Explorers suffer for sufferers

a IN the winter of 1992 two British explorers, Sir Ranulph Fiennes and Dr Michael Stroud, became the first to attempt to cross the Antarctic without the support of dogs or machines. Sir Ranulph was 48, Dr Stroud was 37, and for nearly three months they walked alone across the most inhospitable region on earth.

b The excuse of many mountaineers and explorers for doing what they do is still the age-old 'Because it's there!' In this case, it was not only because it was there or because it had never been done before. It was also to help charity. Through donations from sponsors, the two men raised £2 million for the Multiple Sclerosis* Society of Great Britain. (The society helps people who suffer from multiple sclerosis, as well as funding research into the disease and a possible cure.)

c They set out on 9th November from their base in Gould Bay and walked towards the South Pole, which they reached on January 16, 1993. That in itself was an amazing achievement, as theirs was what is known as an 'unsupported trek'. Put simply, they did it without the help of dogs or vehicles of any kind.

d But then, pulling their sleds further south, within three weeks they had broken the record for the longest polar trek — 1,275 miles in 88 days. And then only a few days after that, they achieved another record — the first unsupported land-mass crossing.

e No expedition like this, however, is without its dangers. By the end, not only had they both lost a third of their body weight, but Dr Stroud had severe frostbite in one hand and Sir Ranulph had frostbite in one foot. Sir Ranulph actually lost about 31kg on the expedition; Dr Stroud lost just over 25 kg.

f They abandoned their trek across Antarctica on February 11. After walking some 1,350 miles unaided in 95 days, they radioed in to report that they were 'more dead than alive'. They were 350 miles from their final destination when an expedition aircraft flew out to take them off the ice. ❄

	Paragraph
1 Two ex-mountaineers faced the Antarctic alone.	☐ 1
2 They broke records all the way.	☐ 2
3 Multiple sclerosis sufferers will benefit from the explorers' suffering.	☐ 3
4 They had to be rescued before achieving their final goal.	☐ 4
5 This hazardous expedition was the direct result of a bet.	☐ 5
6 Two explorers traversed Antarctica unsupported.	☐ 6
7 They were both suffering dreadfully by the end of the expedition.	☐ 7
8 It took them just over two months to walk to the Pole.	☐ 8

* **multiple sclerosis** a disease with an unknown cause, in which an important covering around the nerves is reduced over a period of time, causing more and more difficulties in movement and control of bodily actions (*Longman Modern English Dictionary*)

SECTION C: ENGLISH IN USE

Time: 40 minutes

1 Which of the forms listed can be used to complete the sentence in each case? There may be a number of correct answers. Circle them.

1 He decided to buy a car . . . . have to walk everywhere.

  A so as not to   B to get out of   C so that he wouldn't

  D in order not to   E in case he didn't   F as a precaution against

  G not to

2 . . . . half the people we spoke to agreed with us.

  A Round   B Approximately   C About   D In the order

  E Round about   F Roughly   G Like   H Something like

3 . . . . people nowadays bother to look out for their elderly neighbours.

  A Not much   B Very few   C Only a small number of

  D A small minority   E Not very many   F Very little

4 The old church . . . . while we were there last year.

  A was rebuilt   B had been rebuilt   C has been rebuilt

  D was being rebuilt   E would be rebuilt   F used to be rebuilt

5 We . . . . to the same island for our summer holiday ever since I was five.

  A were going   B have gone   C had gone   D have been going

  E went

6 . . . . rushing out to buy a book the moment it's published. I always wait for the paperback edition.

  A I can't see any point in   B Is it any use   C It's pointless

  D It's not worth   E What's the value   F It's no good

  G What's the sense

7 Although it was a bit complicated, he . . . . solving the problem.

  A succeeded in   B managed to   C had little difficulty in

  D could   E just failed to   F had very little trouble

8 It's about time . . . . about this ridiculous situation!

  A we did something   B something was done

  C we do something   D something is being done

  E we will do something   F something is done

  G we are doing something   H something will be done

2 Read the letter at the top of page 61 and then, in the following items, circle the letter next to the word which best fits each space. The first has been done as an example.

Dear Pat,

I'm sorry I haven't answered your last letter until now, but I've had a lot on my
(0)...... since I got back from my latest business (1)...... to the Far East. Of course
there's nothing like (2)...... for (3)...... your horizons, but in my present (4)......, I
seem to be off on some journey somewhere almost every week. I shouldn't complain
— I managed to (5)...... a fantastic deal for the firm in Hong Kong — but when I get
back home I'm finding it more and more difficult to (6)....... There's always a (7)......
of post waiting to be answered and, of course, the inevitable messages on my
answerphone asking me to contact my head of (8)...... the moment I can. Travelling
round the world is supposed to be one of the (9)...... of the job, but I just don't know.
In the (10)...... you begin to wonder what it's all for!

0	A brain	B head	Ⓒ mind	D thought
1	A trip	B travels	C voyage	D crossing
2	A travel	B journey	C flight	D travels
3	A opening	B spreading	C broadening	D lengthening
4	A vocation	B job	C appointment	D labour
5	A pull off	B hit off	C pay off	D come off
6	A set off	B ring off	C cut off	D switch off
7	A bunch	B pack	C crowd	D pile
8	A warehouse	B company	C department	D factory
9	A pensions	B perks	C commissions	D shares
10	A last	B time	C end	D after

3 This is part of a draft speech which the director of a winter
holiday company, 'Sno-trek', is to give to a group of shareholders.
The board has decided that the director should emphasise the
company itself more by using more passive constructions. On a
separate piece of paper, rewrite just the parts underlined beginning
with the word(s) given in brackets, as in the example below.

People are constantly asking me (0 I ....) how the company is doing. Two years ago
they were heralding our company (1 our company ....) as the most promising in our
field, and they gave us a European Industries Award (2 we ....) for excellence. This
year, unfortunately, our competitors are leaving Sno-trek behind (3 Sno-trek ....).
Certain companies have overtaken us (4 We ....) in promotion and advertising, and
other companies are beating us (5 we ....) in certain European countries. Why is this?
And what can we do about it? (6 what can be ....) I suggest first of all that we should
re-evaluate our promotional activities (7 our promotional ....) and that we give our
designers more scope (8 our designers ....). Furthermore, we are not giving our
representatives in the market (9 our representatives ....) enough support. Until quite
recently we had always provided them (10 they ....) with plenty of material.

0 *I am constantly being asked*

16 Body matters

Grammar

A Re-write the sentences using one of these phrases.

> the odds are …　　　　the chances are …
>
> there's every likelihood …
>
> it's highly (un)likely …
>
> she's/he's (un)likely to …
>
> there's a (strong) chance …

0 He may well be having his operation tomorrow.
   The odds are he'll be having his operation tomorrow.

1 It will probably take him some time to recover from the operation.

   . . . .

   . . . .

2 If you do a lot of sport you are bound to have the occasional injury.

   . . . .

   . . . .

3 She will probably recover in time for the concert.

   . . . .

   . . . .

4 It is probable that no two doctors will treat this rare condition in the same way.

   . . . .

   . . . .

5 People often eventually suffer from the same illnesses as their parents.

   . . . .

   . . . .

6 It's quite likely that she'll pick up some strange infection there.

   . . . .

   . . . .

B Fill in the blanks using the information given in brackets but avoid using a relative pronoun (*who, which, that*).

0 *People suffering from back pain* . . . .
   . . . . should sleep on a hard mattress.
   (People who suffer from back pain)

1 . . . .
   . . . . need to be cared for in special units.
   (Babies who are born very prematurely)

2 Special shoes are made for . . . .
   . . . .
   (people who have arthritis in their feet.)

3 Most of my friends prefer going to . . . .
   . . . .
   (restaurants which specialise in vegetarian food.)

4 . . . .
   . . . . would be well advised to go to their doctor.
   (Anyone who notices an unusual lump in their body)

5 . . . .
   . . . . should take care on the beach.
   (People who are not used to the sun)

6 . . . .
   . . . . should wear protective clothing.
   (People who are likely to be exposed to radioactivity at work)

C Look at the following pieces of first aid advice. In each case the writer has made a grammatical mistake in the advice formula used. Correct it. Write your answers on a separate piece of paper.

0 If you burn your hand, you are recommended putting it in cold water.
   … recommended to put it in cold water.

1 If someone has a black eye, you ought put something cold on it.

2 If a child has eaten poisonous berries, you'd better to take him to a doctor.

3 If someone is unconscious, the first thing to do is putting him in the recovery position.

4 If you think someone may have broken a rib, you must to keep him still.

5 We'd advise that anyone with a serious problem to go to a casualty department.

6 Don't forget checking your home first-aid kit regularly.

Reading

D Look at the titles of health-related magazine articles below and predict what the articles will be about. Write your answers on a separate piece of paper.

0
> # AIDS cure at hand

It will be about the possibility of a cure for AIDS in the near future.

1
> # POP STAR'S BUNDLE OF JOY

2
> # BEAT the BLUES

3
> # Pensioner passes away

4
> # Fencing helps fight flab

5
> # Pizza parlour hygiene row

6
> # Dislocated shoulder stops game

7
> # Better than counting sheep

8
> # Is your building sick?

E The underlined phrases in this text have got confused. For example, (d) should be in space (0). Sort them out.

> Doctors in a number of cities are being encouraged to prescribe a daily dose of swimming in the local pool rather (0) *∂* .. (a) recover from a variety of complaints. It is claimed that five lengths of breast-stroke is (1) .... (b) it usually gives the swimmer as any tablets. Swimming is said to help patients (2) .... (c) this would enable medical staff ranging from flu to stomach disorders. It is thought that the health-restoring faculties (3) .... (d) than a spoonful of medicine its power to improve muscle tone throughout the body as well as from the fact that (4) .... (e) not only by cutting down a general feeling of well-being. Health administrators hope that swimming prescriptions will save money for the Health Service (5) .... (f) of swimming stem from on costs of medicine but also by reducing the queues in doctors' waiting rooms; (6) .... (g) at least as beneficial to spend more time with patients needing less straightforward medical help.

Vocabulary

F Do these two puzzles. The words highlighted in the down columns will be two things a doctor might take for you.

1 Situation where things are not evenly balanced. Anagram ACE IN BALM. (9)

2 If cats make you come out in a rash or start sneezing, you are _ _ _ _ _ _ _ _ to them. (8)

3 He felt a sudden s h _ _ t _ n _ pain and wondered if he was having a heart attack. (8)

4 A noun from 'tense'. (7)

5 To put a joint out of place. Anagram OILED CATS. (9)

6 You must tell the doctor about your s _ _ _ _ _ _ _ before she/he can make a diagnosis. (8)

7 It's what doctors do when they write instructions for the chemist. (9)

8 Blood has white and red ones. Prisoners live in them. Re-order LESCL. (5)

9 Being a pilot is very _ _ _ _ _ _ _ _ _work. An adjective from 'stress'. (9)

10 Another word for backbone. (5)

11 If you are r _ _ d _ _ n, then the doctor might give you a tonic. (7)

12 You feel l _ _ _ _ _ _ _ c when you haven't got the energy to do anything. (9)

13 The noun from 'infectious'. (9)

14 Gymnastics at school is sometimes called _ _ _ s _ _ _ l education. (8)

15 Noun meaning excess. Anagram IETURFS. (7)

16 A colloquial word meaning problems or difficulties and beginning with 'H'. (7)

17 The _ _ _ _ _ _ in the word 'diagnosis' falls on the third syllable. Re-order SSSERT. (6)

18 What you might decide to go on if you want to lose weight. Anagram EDIT. (4)

The doctor might take your _ _ _ _ _ _ _ _ _ _ _ _ and your _ _ _ _ _ .

Writing

G Write a letter giving health advice to a 19-year-old zoology student who is going on a three-month expedition to a very remote place. First decide where she or he is going. Then use this brief plan. Write about 250 words.

1 Opening greetings

2 Preparations before setting off

3 What to take with you

4 How to take care while away

5 Closing wishes

17 Love makes the world go round

Grammar

A Which of the words in the box (**a–l**) will fit sensibly in the blanks in these sentences? There may be a number of possibilities. Write the letters in the blanks.

0 There was hardly . . *f* . . I knew at the party.

1 Can you tell me . . . . . about the new teacher?

2 . . . . . ever tells me what's going on!

3 I didn't like . . . . . of the people my parents invited.

4 They had . . . . . at all to eat for two days.

5 There were . . . . . people she knew at the disco.

6 . . . . . must know who she's going out with!

7 I'll sleep . . . . . at all — even on the floor!

8 It's so boring here. There's . . . . . to go.

9 I didn't like . . . . . shoes in the shop.

10 Can you find . . . . . for us to give them as an engagement present?

11 Ask . . . . . in the village. They *all* know Mark.

12 She told him not to go . . . . . near the main road.

13 . . . . . they could say would persuade me.

14 . . . . . amount of argument would persuade me to marry him.

15 Is there . . . . . I can do to help?

16 Isn't there . . . . . we can do to help?

17 There's always . . . . . to turn to about a problem like this.

18 . . . . . could have told her she was doing the wrong thing.

a	some
b	someone/ somebody
c	something
d	somewhere
e	any
f	anyone/ anybody
g	anything
h	anywhere
i	no
j	no one/ nobody
k	nothing
l	nowhere

B In the dialogues below, B is trying to buy some gadgets. Complete the dialogues like the example and using the prompt words. Write your sentences on a separate piece of paper.

0 A: Can I help you?

  B: (look for/thing/cork/wine bottle)

  Yes, I'm looking for a thing for getting the cork out of a wine bottle.

  or **Yes, I'm looking for a thing I can get the cork out of a wine bottle with.**

  or **Yes, I'm looking for a thing to get the cork out of a wine bottle with.**

  A: Oh, you mean a corkscrew.

1 A: What do you want?

  B: (need/thing/grate/cheese)

  A: Oh, you mean a cheese grater.

2 A: What are you looking for?

  B: (look for/something/keep/cutlery)

  A: Oh, you mean a cutlery box.

3 A: Can I help you?

  B: (want/thingumajig/get core out of apple)

  A: Oh, you mean an apple corer.

4 A: What are you looking for?

  B: (need/tool/undo nuts)

  A: Oh, you mean a spanner.

Vocabulary

C Study these nouns from phrasal verbs. Why are they in two groups, **1** and **2**?

> **1** backwash, downfall, input, intake, offspring, onlooker, onset, outbreak, outcast, outcome, outlet, outlook, upkeep, uprising, uproar, upturn

> **2** breakdown, break-out, cast-offs, cover-up, crackdown, feedback, handout, hold-up, lay-off, letdown, lie-in, look-out, printout, setback, set-up, slip-up, throwback, turnover, turn-up, walkout

Now find words in the box that mean:
1 result, 2 rebellion, 3 disappointment, 4 mistake, 5 forecast, 6 start, 7 delay, 8 children.

Style and register

D Rewrite these sentences, using one of the nouns from the boxes in (**C**) above, and making any other changes necessary.

0 Our car's broken down.
   We've had a breakdown. ....

1 I'll hand out copies to everyone.

   ....

2 I'll print it out and send it to you.

   ....

3 Hundreds have broken out of the high-security prison.

   ....

4 There were very few people looking on.

   ....

5 Someone held up the bank.

   ....

6 Cholera has broken out in the area.

   ....

7 Someone's slipped up again.

   ....

8 I wanted to lie in on Sunday.

   ....

E Newspaper headlines often use 'phrasal verb nouns'. On a separate piece of paper, write what these headlines mean *without* using the underlined nouns.

0
> # Singer's marriage plans face <u>setback</u>

0 *A (famous?) singer's plans to get married have had to be delayed.*

1
> # <u>Outcome</u> of talks uncertain

2
> # Police promise <u>crackdown</u> on crime

3
> # PRESIDENT DENIES <u>COVER-UP</u>

4
> # More <u>lay-offs</u> in the coal industry

5
> # <u>Upturn</u> in economy promised soon

6
> # MASS <u>WALKOUT</u> IN DOCKS

Reading and Writing

F

1 Read this passage and then do exercises 2 and 3 below.

Love sells coffee and chocolates — or does it?

IF PLAYING ON people's fear of death can sell life insurance, if playing on people's desires to succeed can sell educational courses, then in all probability appealing to people's desire for love and romance will sell coffee, or chocolates, or anything. But will it?

There is a saying in English: 'Love me, love my dog'. Nowadays, anyone who watches television commercials might be tempted to rephrase it as 'Love my ad, love my coffee — or my chocolate — or my ...'. Advertisers have always recognised the power of human emotions, but nowadays, it seems, they believe that love and romance are what sell things. Scenes of couples walking hand in hand through the autumn leaves or gazing into each other's eyes in front of a coal fire appear all too often in British television ads. But there are two types.

On the one hand, we have a series of unconnected incidents in which the athletic and ardent lover parachutes from a plane, leaps into a speedboat and roars across a moonlit lake, and finally flies through his mistress's bedroom in order to deliver a box of her favourite brand of chocolates before escaping down the cliff on a rope and jumping back into the speedboat to roar off into the sunset.

On the other, however, one of the most successful campaigns in recent years is the one which is an advertising 'soap' — a soap opera in miniature, if you like. A man and a woman living in adjoining apartments meet when he knocks on her door to ask if she has any coffee. He has run out. Of course she has some coffee. He keeps running out, there is a clear physical attraction (for each other, not the coffee!), and eventually they fall in love — and it's all down to 'X' brand of coffee — for that's what brought them together in the first place.

So does either sell a product? Or do they just have a viewing audience the same as any other series or soap opera? I suspect it's the latter, and that while the advertisers think they're helping to sell more coffee or chocolates, all they are really doing is producing serial or soap-opera stories shorter than, but as good as anything else the viewer can watch.

2 Summarise in about 50 words the points the writer makes.

3 Write a letter to the magazine which published the above article. Comment on it. Then describe two or more advertisements you have seen which use love or other strong emotions to try to sell something and comment on how effective you feel the ads are. You should try to write about 250 words.

18 There's no accounting for taste

Grammar

A Rewrite these sentences, using the word given (in brackets) after each one.

0 I enjoy playing tennis much more than watching it. (PREFER)
   I much prefer playing tennis to watching it.

1 I can't stand being talked about behind my back. (PEOPLE)

....

2 I'd rather go to the exhibition than the concert. (PREFER)

....

3 I'd prefer you not to say anything. (RATHER)

....

4 Why did you go and tell him? (WISH)

....

5 Saying this is painful, but I'm afraid you're not up to it. (HATE)

....

6 The idea of getting old worries me because of the effect it has on your mind. (WHAT)

....

7 It was so horrible I had to turn away. (BEAR)

....

8 I like everything about the CAE except the time limits. (ONLY)

....

B This is an extract from a reference for an employee that your boss has written. He has totally lost confidence in his use of prepositions. Help him. Fill in the missing prepositions.

Mr Martin is someone (0) *for* whom I have the highest personal regard. In the five years he has worked (1)........ this company, he has displayed an exemplary attitude (2)........ all facets of his work.

He has a real flair (3)........ person-management. He takes a genuine interest (4)........ his staff, takes care (5)........ their professional requirements and even looks (6)........ their social and domestic needs. He has the happy gift (7)........ being able to get on well (8)........ everyone. I can honestly not recall one member of staff (9)........ whom he has not hit it off, so to speak.

He is not only an expert [10]....... his field, he is also expert [11]....... passing his expertise [12]....... to others. He has an engagingly calm manner, never one to make a fuss [13]....... things that go wrong, capable [14]....... taking everything in his stride.

Mr Martin takes great pride [15]....... his appearance and has immaculate taste [16]....... clothes. His attendance record is second [17]....... none and his achievements have earned him the respect [18]....... all our staff, who regard him rightly [19]....... a model colleague.

I am sure he would succeed [20]....... bringing to your organisation the same level of commitment as he has shown here and I would commend him to you [21].......reservation.

Style and register

C Read the text on the left, then complete the one on the right, which gives identical advice but in a more formal style. Decide on one word only for each gap.

Of course, everyone knows that you've got to have insurance on your things. But not many people realise what these things are really worth. So lots of people are seriously underinsured.

You really ought to make a list of everything you've got that's worth £20 or more, remembering that it's what it would cost you to replace it *now* that's important.

If I were you, I'd check out what present prices are. You could usefully ask an expert about antiques and things like glass.

Don't wait! Why not start your list today? And then get in touch with your broker immediately.

You won't be sorry!

You value your possessions — but do you appreciate how they have appreciated in value?

It is, of course, common [0] *knowledge*....... that it is absolutely [1]..................... to [2]..................... out an insurance policy on one's [3]..................... Very [4].................. people, [5]..................., are aware of their true [6]..................... [7]....................., the vast [8]..................... of people possess [9]..................... cover. It is [10].................. to draw up a list of items worth in [11]................. of £20, [12]..................... in mind that it is the cost of [13]..................... at today's prices that [14]..................... You would be well [15]..................... to consult up-to-date price lists. It might be an [16]..................... to seek professional [17]..................... in the [18]..................... of antiques and [19]..................... items as glassware. Delay could be disastrous. There is no time like the [20]..................... to [21]..................... a start. When you have completed your list, [22]..................... your insurance broker without [23]..................... You will not [24]..................... it.

Vocabulary

D Below are some words and phrases which rhyme with adjectives we use to describe something or someone we like, and words and phrases which rhyme with adjectives we use to describe someone or something we dislike. What are the adjectives? The first one in each group has been done for you.

Complimentary words		Uncomplimentary words	
0 inactive	*attractive*	0 vastly	*ghastly*
1 elephant	....	1 falling	....
2 ceiling	....	2 bed full	....
3 new verb	....	3 no desk	....
4 ended	....	4 tremendous	....
5 present	....	5 lawful	....
6 hate	....	6 fastidious	....

Writing

E This is an extract from a mail-order catalogue you were sent some time ago. You liked the sound of some of the items and wrote to order them. The disappointment you felt when you received the goods is reflected in the handwritten comments you made in the brochure. Write now to the company, complaining about the articles and asking either for replacements or a full refund.

BARGAINS

Just a few of the once-in-a-lifetime bargains that could be yours

2 were cracked, 1 chipped

★ exquisitely hand-painted dinner plates (set of 6) **£24.99**

Handle came off one as I took it out of the box – a joke!

★ robust pots for your favourite mouth-watering dishes (set of 3) **£34.99**

Pen simply doesn't write!

★ beautifully crafted pen and pencil set, a joy forever **£19.95**

Pair they sent 2 sizes too small!

★ pair of trainers (please indicate size and colour) **£31.50**

Can't assemble. 2 screws missing, bars different length. Holes too big.

★ unique real-wood stacking for CDs and videos (self-assembly) **£16.49**

Show completely different weight if I weigh same thing twice.

★ precision kitchen scales, accurate to within 5 gm. (in red, white or black) **£25.49**

I didn't read what it said!

Grammar

A Is the word order in the following sentences correct or not? If it is, just tick in the space provided. If not, circle the word in the wrong place and indicate with an arrow where it should be.

0 Perhaps ~~should~~ the paper be folded in half first. . . . . .

1 Never has so much been done for so many by so few. . . . . .

2 Under no circumstances I would do what he suggests. . . . . .

3 No sooner had he finished one car than he started servicing the next. . . . . .

4 Next should the vegetables be chopped before marinating overnight. . . . . .

5 Only if you keep the oven door closed during cooking will the cake rise properly. . . . . .

6 Only after I had been learning to drive for six weeks did I begin to feel I was mastering it. . . . . .

7 It was not until had they arrived at the airport that they remembered their passports. . . . . .

8 Never I can understand how technical things work. . . . . .

B Fill each of the gaps in this text with an appropriate conjunction or connector.

(0) **Although** I enjoy cooking, I have frequently had disasters in the kitchen. Once long ago, in the days (1). . . . . garlic was still a novelty in England, I got confused between a clove and a head, (2). . . . . put an entire head into a cucumber and yoghurt salad. It looked so cool and delicious (3). . . . . all my guests took large helpings. Rarely can they have had a greater shock (4). . . . . when they took their first mouthful. On another occasion I decided to bake some 'quick and easy' bread (5). . . . . we had none in the house (6). . . . . guests were invited for dinner. Being in a hurry, I decided (7). . . . . there was no need to weigh everything exactly and (8). . . . . I just guessed how much of the ingredients to use. I suppose it is not surprising (9). . . . . the loaf was as hard as a rock and had much the same taste. Never have I been quite so embarrassed, (10). . . . . , as (11). . . . . I offered my guests salt instead of sugar with their coffee. This happened (12). . . . . my little boy had heard that sugar was bad for you and had decided to fill the sugar bowl with something less harmful for the teeth!

Vocabulary

C Choose one of the verbs from this box to complete each of the sentences below. Put each verb into an appropriate form.

> scald   simmer   stir   whisk   freeze ✓ rub   scrub   scratch
> wipe   dip   graze

0   The water in the tank . . *froze* . . . , later bursting the pipes when it thawed.

1   I know your mosquito bites itch but do try not to . . . . them.

2   . . . . your elbow in the bathwater before you put the baby in.

3   Take care with that boiling water — you might . . . . yourself.

4   Keep . . . . the custard while it is cooking.

5   Let the soup . . . . for about five minutes and then it will be ready to eat.

6   When she had stopped crying, he gave her a tissue and she . . . . her eyes.

7   Omelettes are deliciously light if you . . . . the mixture before cooking it.

8   The kitchen floor was so dirty after the party that it took me ages . . . . it clean.

9   Little children are constantly falling over and . . . . their knees.

10 She . . . . her hair with a towel until it was almost dry.

D What categories do each of these groups of words fall into? Add two more words to each category.

0 stapler, paper clip, hole punch
   Office equipment — correcting fluid, sellotape . . . .

1 grater, colander, ladle
   . . . .

2 pliers, hammer, screwdriver
   . . . .

3 spark plugs, dipstick, battery
   . . . .

4 jar, tube, carton
   . . . .

5 rake, secateurs, spade
   . . . .

6 VDU, disk, printer
   . . . .

a . . . .   e . . . .
b . . . .   f . . . .
c . . . .   g . . . .
d . . . .   h . . . *bell* . . . .

i . . . .   l . . . .
j . . . .   m . . . .
k . . . .

E Label the parts of the bike.

handlebars   bell ✓   brake   spokes   pedals   wheel   saddle
pump   tyre   crossbar   mudguard   light   chain

Reading

F These instructions about how to play draughts are in the wrong order. What order should they be in? The first and last are given to help you.

a ..... The players decide who will have each colour and black always starts.

b ..... Ordinary men, moving forwards, can capture kings.

c ..... One man can jump over more than one of the opponent's men in one turn providing all jumps are made over one man at a time to a vacant square and in a diagonally forward direction.

d ..... The king can now move, or capture, both forwards and backwards, in any subsequent turn.

e ..... If a man reaches the opposite side of the board, another man of the same colour (one that has been removed from the board) is placed on top to form a 'king'.

f ..1.. The aim of the game of draughts is to take all of the opponent's men.

g ..... If the square diagonally forward is occupied by an opponent's man and the square beyond is free then it is possible to jump over the opponent's man to the free square, removing the opponent's man from the board.

h ..... Each player takes the twelve men of their colour and places them on the black squares of the three rows nearest to them.

i ..12.. A player has won when he has taken all of his opponent's men or when those that are left cannot move.

j ..... Players take turns to move one square forward diagonally.

k ..... This board should be placed between the two players so that the bottom square to the left of each player is a black one.

l ..... The game is played by two players on a chequered board.

G There is an extra word in some of the lines of this text. Some lines are correct. Circle the extra words and tick in the space provided the lines that are correct.

0 Shirley Conran recommends that women should (to) take regular care of their cars in   .....

1 the same way they do their faces. She particularly advises on joining a Motoring   .....

2 Association as these can help you out at any time of the day or night not whenever   .....

3 you have a problem. Apart from that she urges drivers to carry out weekly checks   .....

4 on their cars looking in most particular at battery, plugs, radiator and oil. She points   .....

5 out that any smell of burning in a car should be investigated into at once as it could   .....

6 be a portent of something both dangerous and expensive. Not only can burning smells   .....

7 but also a steaming radiator can be the sign of a serious problem. Stop the car at once   .....

8 and check the engine if either of symptom suddenly appears.   .....

Writing

H Choose one of these and write precise instructions (for a young person) on how to do it:

a) play dominoes; b) do a somersault; c) use a tape-recorder;
d) ride a bike.

2C Into the future!

Grammar

start work in new job
go to Los Angeles
verdict given ✓
stand at the altar
get married
stand in court ✓
leave present company
land in California
sit in the aeroplane
finish last paper
set off on honeymoon
take final college exams
go on trial ✓
clear desk
sit in examination hall

Writing

A You are going to think about the week ahead for five different people. First, group the prompts into sets of three according to subject. Then put them into their natural time order: 1) *am/is/are doing*, 2) *will/may/might be doing*, 3) *will/may/might have done*. Finally, expand each group into a complete view of one person's week to come. Use the tenses 1–3 as in the example.

0   *A neighbour of mine is going on trial for burglary on Monday. This time next week I suppose he'll be standing in court trying to prove his innocence. By the end of the week I expect the verdict will have been given and he may well be starting quite a long prison sentence.*

B Here are some notes on how technology is changing and will change our driving habits. Use them to write an article entitled 'The Road to the Future'.

ALREADY	SOON	ONE DAY
■ Computers taking over drivers' work, assessing/recording car's performance	■ Computers to judge correct distance from car in front; radar sensors to adjust distance	■ Computers to programme journey — drivers do little or nothing
■ Spoken messages of warning and information	■ Alarm systems to warn of danger	■ Self-correcting engine and other parts
■ Under-garden garages (under lawn or drive) to reduce thefts and prevent corrosion	■ Sensors to detect when driver unfit for driving — too sleepy, etc. — automatic dispensing of perfumes and switching on of air-conditioning to keep driver awake	■ Petrol fill and payment without driver leaving car

Your first sentence could be: **A major revolution has already started in what we drive and how we drive it.**

Register and vocabulary

C Here are some of the things that you, as staff representative, were recently tempted to say to your boss on behalf of your colleagues. Instead you decided to put pen to paper. Follow this example and complete the sentences on page 75.

0   **You thought:** Do you honestly expect us to work on Saturdays?
   You wrote: In our opinion it is absurd that *we should be expected to work on Saturdays.*

1 You don't really think we're going to take a cut in salary, do you?
  We feel that it is ridiculous that . . . .
  . . . .

2 We're not looking for trouble and that's that.
  There is not a grain . . . .
  . . . .

3 There's nothing odd about us wanting better working conditions.
  It is only natural that . . . .
  . . . .

4 If you don't come up with a better offer, we're out on strike, OK?
  Unless management is prepared . . . .
  . . . .

5 You can put it down to world recession, but you won't talk us out
  of strike action.
  You may try to explain . . . .
  . . . .

6 So you're going to try and crack down on absence? You haven't
  got a hope!
  Your attempts to . . . .
  . . . .

7 Just because you've got a spot of bother with your suppliers, don't
  try and take it out on us.
  We do not feel it is right . . . .
  . . . .

Now write here what you thought before you wrote these lines to
your employer:

8 Basically it all boils . . . .
  . . . .

  We feel it is ultimately a question of mutual trust.
9 You can't talk us . . . .
  . . . .

  We are not prepared to give up our rights in this matter.
10 You've got to face up . . . .
  . . . .

  It is ludicrous to think that any of us will accept voluntary
  redundancy.
11 We're not going to put . . . .
  . . . .

  We are not prepared to tolerate this situation any longer.

Reading

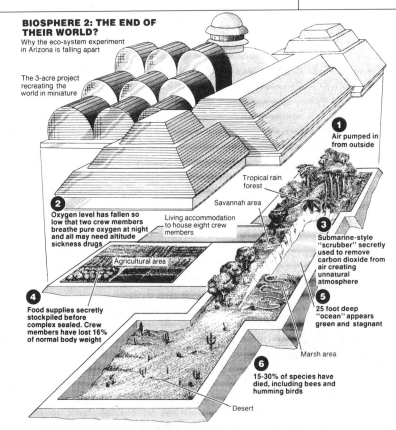

D In this text some phrases have been left out and appear below. Decide which phrases go where and write the numbers (0 – 10) beside the letters (**a – n**). Three phrases are not needed.

BIOSPHERE 2: THE END OF THEIR WORLD?

Why the eco-system experiment in Arizona is falling apart

The 3-acre project recreating the world in miniature

1 Air pumped in from outside

2 Oxygen level has fallen so low that two crew members breathe pure oxygen at night and all may need altitude sickness drugs

Tropical rain forest

Savannah area

Living accommodation to house eight crew members

Agricultural area

3 Submarine-style "scrubber" secretly used to remove carbon dioxide from air creating unnatural atmosphere

4 Food supplies secretly stockpiled before complex sealed. Crew members have lost 16% of normal body weight

5 25 foot deep "ocean" appears green and stagnant

Marsh area

6 15-30% of species have died, including bees and humming birds

Desert

Future imperfect

After just twelve of its planned twenty-four months' duration, the much-heralded Biosphere 2 experiment was hitting severe snags and facing a far from certain future. By Christmas 1992, many experts were suggesting that it would not last another twelve weeks, (0)......

The mission was set up in the Arizona desert, (1)....., in a blaze of publicity in late 1991, with a view to exploring the possibility of colonisation of other planets. It involved eight people living in a sealed environment, a miniature self-sufficient world containing (2)..... to rainforest, agricultural areas to desert. The aim was to prove that such a colony could exist healthily and happily for two years; (3).....

After just one year, some of the crew were suffering from tiredness and lethargy, (4)..... The air was so thin (5)..... that several needed a daily intake of pure oxygen; (6)...... After a poor harvest, all crew members had lost up to 16% of their body weight.

The ocean had gone green (7)..... 3,800 species of flora and fauna had been present at the outset; after a year about 20% of the plants had gone, (8)..... The bees and humming birds had disappeared almost completely; (9).....

A spokesperson for the group admitted at the time that there had been problems: 'We never expected things to go that smoothly; (10)......'.

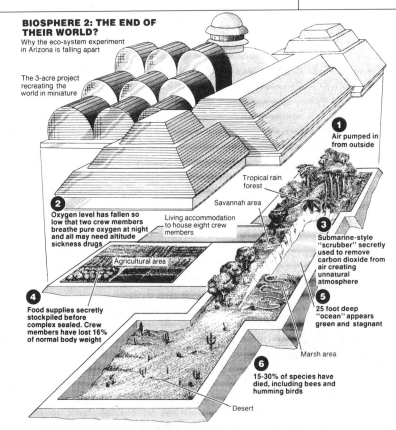 * See note on inside front cover.

..... **a** everything from ocean

..... **b** while even more animals had died

..... **c** apart from the oxygen problem

..... **d** and was full of thick sludge

..... **e** however, things went badly wrong

..... **f** on the other hand it has given us the chance to do some serious scientific research

..... **g** not to mention insomnia

..... **h** some indeed were already on altitude sickness tablets

..**0**.. **i** let alone months

..... **j** whereas it had been mainly successful

..... **k** and of such poor quality

..... **l** you may recall

..... **m** pollination of plants, therefore, had virtually ceased

..... **n** unlike things from the ocean

Progress Test 4 (Units 16–20)

SECTION A: WRITING

Time: 45 minutes

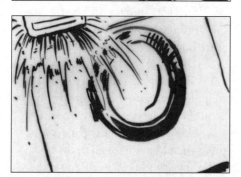

You have just returned from a holiday with some friends. Together you rented a holiday villa, the 'Villa Rosanne', near the sea. Here are three short extracts from the instructions that you found when you arrived.

■ To use the washing machine:

1 Put clothes in — for best results, only half-fill the drum.

2 Put washing-powder in the detergent compartment at the top left-hand side and close compartment.

3 Select the programme you require.

4 Press the green button to start.

5 The machine stops automatically at the end of the programme.

■ Watering plants:

The plants in pots on the patio should be watered each evening.

Water the hanging baskets morning and evening.

■ On leaving, please lock all windows, lock the front and back doors securely and leave the villa keys with Mr Dean at the local store.

Unfortunately, not everything was that simple. Things went wrong.

Referring to the instructions and to the holiday pictures, write an apologetic letter to the owner of the villa (Mrs Ginelli) explaining everything that happened and offering to pay for any serious damage caused. By the way, you found the keys to the villa in your bag when you got home. Write 200–250 words.

SECTION B: READING

Suggested time: 15 minutes

Read this and answer questions 1–6 below.

'Keep Fit' videos

What they are — and what you think

'Keep Fit' is booming in many countries, and so is the sale of Keep Fit, 'Workout' or Aerobics videos. A 'Keep Fit' video is one which shows a number of exercises performed to music by someone (often famous) for you to do at the same time. Many people benefit from working out at home in front of the TV without having to go out to the local sports centre, but there may be a hidden price to pay for leaping about in time with your chosen 'Keep Fit god or goddess' on film. We asked a number of people what they thought of Keep Fit videos. Here is a selection of opinions.

a   You never know what too much strenuous physical exercise like this might do to a person's body — not only muscles, but internal organs too. I can't actually *prove* any connection in any one case, but some of the surgery I've had to perform has, in my opinion, been the direct result of over-exercise.

b   I've heard that in some cases too much exercise can result in chronic joint problems later in life. But I'm really fit. I've never felt any pain in any of my joints. I don't think I ever will. And I do about half an hour every day with the video I bought. I actually miss it if I don't do it.

c   If you suffer from any sort of back trouble, I think you'd be asking for trouble doing some of these exercises. I might be coming up for fifty, but I've had a bad back for years, and as long as I'm not stupid, I'm fine. The best exercise for me is walking in the fresh air — not jumping up and down in front of the TV set!

d   You'd never believe the results I've seen in my surgery — twisted ankles, stiff legs, sprained wrists, stiff necks, chronic backache …! It's quite clear that many of the exercises put the spine under too much pressure.

e   I'm sure keeping fit at home like this for us older folks is preferable to doing no exercise at all. Living in the heart of the countryside, there is no way I can get to a gym or sports club. I think they're a marvellous idea.

f   People would incur far fewer sprains and strains if they followed the instructions properly. The trouble is, so many of us just turn on the video and try and copy everything we see. The instructions are quite clear. A video itself can't be dangerous, can it?

g   The advice is always to build up the exercises you do slowly and carefully over a period. Of course I wouldn't have as many patients, but then I have enough to do dealing with injuries caused on the football field and so on.

Which writer(s) or speaker(s):

1 suggests that people don't use Keep Fit videos in the proper way?   ☐ 1

2 suspect that many of their patients sustain injuries from following Keep Fit video exercises? (3 answers)   ☐ ☐ ☐ 2

3 warns middle-aged people about doing these kinds of exercises?   ☐ 3

4 sounds like a young keep-fit enthusiast?   ☐ 4

5 says that Keep Fit videos can take the place of a sports club?   ☐ 5

6 think there is a connection between these exercises and back trouble? (2 answers)   ☐ ☐ 6

SECTION C: ENGLISH IN USE

Time: 40 minutes

1 Read this extract from a novel and then, in the following items, circle the letters next to the word which best fits each space. The first has been done as an example.

As far as Slick could see, there was a very good ⁽⁰⁾..... that he would be promoted to run another branch of the PFF organisation. (PFF was short for Planning For the Future).The ⁽¹⁾..... was good, as the weathermen would say. He ⁽²⁾..... liked the idea of being in charge of an organisation that really *was* ⁽³⁾..... the problems of the future. That was what it was in business for, although it had ⁽⁴⁾..... a good deal of criticism for doing so. Right from the ⁽⁵⁾..... people seemed to think that PFF was a government department and should not be in it for profit. Slick himself, despite his name, would have ⁽⁶⁾..... the organisation to have been less commercial. The previous year, for example, it had had an almost 'immoral' ⁽⁷⁾..... of some £25 million.

Slick leaned back in his chair, ⁽⁸⁾..... his neck where another mosquito had ⁽⁹⁾..... him, took out his handkerchief and ⁽¹⁰⁾..... his brow. There was no difference between winter and summer now. It was always hot.

---

0 A likelihood	Ⓑ chance	C probability	D circumstances
1 A outlook	B outlet	C letdown	D outcast
2 A absolutely	B fairly	C utterly	D rather
3 A coming across as	B facing up to	C putting up with	D coming up against
4 A talked out of	B got round to	C put down to	D come in for
5 A outset	B set-up	C onset	D setback
6 A rather	B longed	C preferred	D wished
7 A upturn	B input	C intake	D turnover
8 A grazed	B scraped	C scratched	D sprinkled
9 A squeezed	B stung	C bitten	D hit
10 A stroked	B scrubbed	C caressed	D wiped

2 Rewrite each of the following sentences beginning with the word or words given on the next line. Your rewritten version should be as close to the original as possible.

1 There's not much likelihood of that happening.

It's . . . .

2 It might be advisable not to mention it to her.

You'd . . . .

3 Shouldn't we knock first before we go in?

Hadn't . . . .

4 We won't get anywhere if we spend so long on each point.

We'll ....

5 I'd rather save my money than spend it on rubbish like that.

I'd prefer ....

6 The moment she finished eating one sweet, she ate another.

No sooner ....

7 Remove all four batteries from the radio and replace with new ones.

All four batteries ....

8 Please don't mention it again.

I'd rather ....

9 I regret never having been to China.

I wish ....

10 Last week he lost his job *and* he lost a lot of money gambling.

Apart from ....

3 In most lines of this text there is one spelling mistake. Read the text, underline each wrongly spelt word and write the correct spelling in the space provided at the end of the line. Where a line is completely correct, put a tick (✓) against the line number.

I first noticed the symptoms when I was cooking a meal last	1 ....
week. I had all the ingredients out on the table and was	2 ....
cruching some garlic when I suddenly began to perspire.	3 ....
And then I remember spesifically holding on to the edge of	4 ....
the table before I fainted. I had had a poor appetite for a few	5 ....
days before that, too. Anyway, I regained consciousness —	6 ....
the garlic suddenly smelled abominible — dragged myself	7 ....
off to bed and rang the doctor: 'Yes, I had a feavour. No,	8 ....
my nose wasn't pooring with blood. (Why should it?) And	9 ....
yes, the inside of my mouth did look horendous!'	10 ....

4 Here are some instructions for putting a roll of thermal paper into a fax machine, written in a formal style. Write a simpler version of the instructions to put by the machine for colleagues in an office. Begin 'Pull the "Open Cover" lever towards you. Lift the cover …' — and maintain this style throughout.

Loading the thermal paper roll

1 The lever marked 'Open Cover' should be pulled towards you and the cover lifted until the weight has been taken by the support arm.

2 The roll of paper must be removed from its wrapping before the former is placed carefully into the shallow compartment.

3 The end of the paper is then fed under the paper guide whence it will be seen to appear under the front of the machine.

4 The cover should then be closed firmly but gently until it clicks into position.

5 The thermal paper will then be fed through by the fax machine and a short length of thermal paper cut off automatically.